The Curti Lectures

The University of Wisconsin–Madison
April 1981

To honor the distinguished historian Merle Curti,
lectures in social and intellectual history
were inaugurated in 1976 under the sponsorship of the
University of Wisconsin Foundation and the
Department of History of the University of Wisconsin–Madison.

Published by the University of Wisconsin Press

Christopher Hill, *Some Intellectual Consequences of the English Revolution* (1980)

Carlo M. Cipolla, *Fighting the Plague in Seventeenth-Century Italy* (1981)

Law and Markets in United States History

Different Modes of Bargaining Among Interests

James Willard Hurst

THE UNIVERSITY OF WISCONSIN PRESS

Published 1982

The University of Wisconsin Press
114 North Murray Street
Madison, Wisconsin 53715

The University of Wisconsin Press, Ltd.
1 Gower Street
London WC1E 6HA, England

First printing

Printed in the United States of America

For LC CIP information see the colophon

ISBN 0-299-09050-7 cloth; 09054-X paper

Contents

Contents

Acknowledgments

I am grateful to my colleagues of the Department of History of the University of Wisconsin for the invitation to deliver the Curti Lectures in April 1981, from which these essays derive. It is especially pleasing thus to be able to share with others in honoring the work by which Merle Curti has over the years contributed so much to our understanding of the value inheritance of this society.

Themes developed here grow out of a long-term program of work in the economic and social history of law in the United States. I am indebted for support in this effort to the Social Science Research Council, the Rockefeller Foundation, the administration of the University of Wisconsin, and most particularly of late years to the trustees of the William F. Vilas Trust Estate, under whose auspices I have held a chair as Vilas Professor of Law at the University of Wisconsin. Of course, the book does not purport to speak for any of these agencies; I take sole responsibility for what I write.

Madison, Wisconsin
August 1981

*Law and Markets
in United States History*

The Market, the Law, and Challenges of Scarcity

People in the United States have shared with all human kind the stubborn limitations that scarcity imposes on life, whether in material goods and services, in power over others, or in emotional fulfillment through other avenues. All our social institutions have functioned to help cope with scarcity of life satisfactions. But the people of the United States have made particularly heavy and pervasive demands on the market and the law to help them come to terms with limits imposed by impersonal physical or biological circumstances or by imperfections in social structure or processes. These essays explore some relationships between market processes and legal processes as the country has sought to use these to respond to challenges of scarcity.

Chapter 1 deals with public policy affecting the existence and functioning of the market as an institution valued particularly for achieving economic efficiency—conceived, in legal terms, as the most output for the least input—by activity of private operators in producing and distributing goods and services for private profit. Chapter 2 examines uses of law to adjust relations among market-measured values and values defined in other than market terms. Chapter 3 focuses on distinctive capacities and limitations of legal processes as means of adjusting diverse and often competing interests, compared with the utility of market processes for comparable ends.

These divisions are for convenience in ordering tangled material. The realities of the subject overlap and intertwine. Consider the range of concerns implicated in determining the scope which public policy should give to freedom of private contract. The law legitimized large freedom of private contract as a functional requisite of the private market—a concern of Chapter 1. But —matters relevant to Chapter 2—public policy had also to weigh how far effective freedom of private contract depended on a healthy social context and must be adjusted to that context. Some measure of private market autonomy—freedom of private contract—figures in the overall separation of powers which our tradition has rated as crucial to the distinctive role of legal processes in allocating scarce resources, examined in Chapter 3. We cannot label freedom of contract simply an element of the private market considered in isolation.[1]

"The market" is a convenient, conventional shorthand term. Diverse realities lie back of the shorthand. A single, all-embracing market no more exists than does the single, standardized, reasonable and prudent individual beloved in tort doctrine. The country's economic history shows many markets. The course of business practice and of public policy has been different regarding markets for products of heavy industry, for distribution of consumer goods, for capital investment, for labor, for insurance, for transportation, for electric power.[2] Yet there is more than a convenient fiction in referring also to "the market." Some important working characteristics are common to many diverse markets, to an extent that has found reflection in public policy.[3] Both the market and markets have in fact been material components of social order in the United States. The two realities were evident in the Supreme Court's treatment of *Nebbia* v. *New York* (1934).[4] Economic depression had wreaked peculiar havoc on New York State's milk industry; disastrous declines in price led farmers to stop the flow of milk from farms to city consumers, with attendant further loss to the farm economy and danger to the well-being of city people. The New York legislature responded by imposing a scheme of price controls designed to halt the economically and socially damaging downspiral of prices. A retailer challenged the price regulations as invading his rights of property and liberty in violation of the due process clause of the Fourteenth Amendment. Upholding the regulations, the Supreme Court measured them against a standard of rationality, in turn measured by what the legislature could reasonably find to be the distinctive problems of the New York milk market. In this aspect the decision reflects the reality of diverse markets, each of which may present to public policy its own special concerns. But Nebbia also raised a broader issue. Freedom of dealers in market to set their own prices was, he argued, historically and in principle a key element to the existence and vitality of all market action; policy tradition had sanctioned legal regulation of prices only in those businesses of special character which history had stamped as public utilities, and in history the milk business had never qualified as a public utility. By his logic it followed that New York's regulatory scheme violated due process of law because it so far departed from the standard rationale of the market as a serviceable social institution. The Supreme Court also rejected this broader attack. The Court affirmed general authority in the legislature to reach reasonable decisions in the public interest on measures it found would maintain market operations in healthy adjustment to the general social context:

> The due process clause makes no mention of sales or of prices any more than it speaks of business or contracts or buildings or other incidents of property. The thought seems nevertheless to have persisted that there is something peculiarly sacrosanct about the price one may charge for what he makes or sells, and that, however able to regulate other elements of manufacture or trade, with incidental effect upon price, the state is incapable of directly controlling the price itself. This view was negatived many years ago. Munn v. Illinois, 94 U.S. 113. . . . This court [there] concluded the circumstances justified the legislation as an exercise of the governmental right to control the business in the public interest.

. . . [T]here is no closed class or category of business affected with
a public interest, and the function of courts in the application of
the Fifth and Fourteenth Amendments is to determine in each case
whether circumstances vindicate the challenged regulation as a
reasonable exertion of governmental authority or condemn it as
arbitrary or discriminatory.[5]

In the United States market dealing has typically been conducted by operators who do not have official status and do not
make their bargaining decisions at the direction of public officers. True, a market is an administrative device that can serve
diverse states of society. Markets are not necessarily associated
with private capitalism; in the twentieth century, socialist countries have allowed some scope for markets for labor and for consumer goods, and in some instances experimented overtly or co-
vertly with bargaining among state enterprises which ap-
proached the transaction styles familiar in a capitalist framework.[6] The nineteenth-century United States showed some
notable exceptions to the ordinarily private character of market
dealing. Some portion of the public domain the United States or
the states sold at auction, and the nation—or states as delegates
of the nation—also bargained out exchange of public lands for
farmers' labor invested in homesteads and for private contractors' construction of turnpikes, canals, and railroads.[7] In war-
time, and in peacetime as governments expanded their service
activities and their funding of technical and scientific research,
government contracts grew to substantial proportions.[8] Indeed,
in the twentieth century such developments made access to contract relations with government of sufficient importance that the
Supreme Court, substantially rejecting older doctrine which
treated such advantageous relations with government as a matter of privilege rather than of right, gave a measure of protection
to such relations under standards of due process and equal protection of law.[9] Overall, however, government involvement in
marketlike bargaining has been the exception. From our na-

tional beginnings into the late twentieth century, market dealing has been dominantly among private persons.

So far as public policy has considered relations of market activity to the general social context, two main areas of concern have appeared. The most obvious departure from a market focus has been the use of law to foster values not measured by market transactions. Especially in statute law and in administrative rules and regulations made under statutory delegation, this emphasis of policy took the form of developing canons of social income and cost accounting.[10] But the prominence of this type of legal intervention did not negate another kind of concern for social context—regard for the general vitality of the private market itself as an institution of social order. As Chapter 1 indicates, law entered into the structure of the market both boldly and in detail in ways primarily significant for advancing specific private transactions. But on occasion public policy has moved to assert an overarching social interest in the vigor and continuity of the market, reaching beyond the focused concerns of particular bargainers, as the Supreme Court did in analyzing the problems posed in *Nebbia* v. *New York*.[11] An accounting of efforts by law to adjust the market to the social context must include attention both to nonmarket values and to the community interest in the institutional integrity of the market itself.

Even when they work imperfectly, market processes are processes of bargaining adjustments of diverse or competing interests. In contrast, the law more often presents a front of command than of bargain.[12] The element of command is particularly to the fore in legal regulation to safeguard nonmarket values from harmful impacts of market-oriented calculations. But to an important degree, the law's appearance of command is misleading. Legal processes, in fact, produce a good deal of adjustment of interests by bargain. Beyond this, in the growth of our legal tradition they have been accepted as legitimately promoting the good order of social relations through bargains managed and consummated by official procedures.[13] As means of bargaining, market processes and legal processes reveal distinctive strengths and weaknesses. Chapter 3 seeks to compare some qualities and defects of both institutions affecting the tone and temper of the social order.

CHAPTER 1

Law and the Constitution of the Market

Trading among private persons for profit was not a creation of law. This became the more obvious as trading grew in volume, in geographical range, in diversity of goods and services exchanged, and in spans of time required for completing transactions. The private market—sustained patterns of private trading for profit—was primarily the product of goals set and means fashioned by industrialists, merchants, bankers, lenders and borrowers, employers and employees, and ultimate consumers. To these various participants in their roles as parties to private bargains the prime function of the market, which warranted it an acceptable institution of social control, was to apply certain and specialized criteria of efficiency in use of scarce economic resources. Relative to the whole play of factors that produced the market, the law was marginal. This is not to say that law was unimportant. In various respects law exerted material leverage on the development and working character of the institution. Assessment of these contributions of law is the business of this essay; the next two chapters examine public policy relevant to the market in respects other than those defined by market-measured efficiency.

PUBLIC POLICY REFLECTIONS OF THE
PRIMACY OF THE MARKET

From the country's national beginnings and well into the twentieth century the market captured people's imagination, energy, and ambition to an extent and with a sustained hold unmatched by any other institution. The early course of public policy reflected this central position of the market in three salient respects: trade, land, and the centrist character of political dealings with conflicts among private economic interests.

In the late eighteenth century in his *Letters from an American Farmer,* Crevecouer praised the open character of life in the United States. He found it a culture which fostered the individual's self-respect through mingled features of the economy and the polity, by giving him access both to freehold land title and to the vote. Crevecouer particularly measured the vital force of the society by the ordinary farmer's capacity to produce for trade:

> Every industrious European who transports himself here, may be compared to a sprout growing at the foot of a great tree; it enjoys and draws but a little portion of sap; wrench it from the parent roots, transplant it, and it will become a tree bearing fruit also. Colonists are therefore entitled to the consideration due to the most useful subjects; a hundred families barely existing in some parts of Scotland, will here in six years, cause an annual exportation of 10,000 bushels of wheat, 100 bushels being but a common quantity for an industrious family to sell, if they cultivate good land.[1]

The more significant because it is so taken for granted is the assumption that these farmers produce wheat "to sell"; the norm is already seen to be, not a subsistence, but a commercial agriculture. Significant, too, is that Crevecouer—not a lawyer—puts his observations in a legal context, in effect assigning key influence to the law of property (freehold land title) and of contract (bargains of sale).

The central concerns of the Federal Constitution were necessarily the structure and security of a new form of government. Otherwise, no area of policy evoked more detail than provisions relevant to dealings in market. To prevent destructive trade wars among states and to assure a central capacity to represent national interest against the competing economic policies of other countries, Congress held power "to regulate commerce with foreign nations, and among the several states." To provide a uniform and reliable money supply, without which trade must stay within the cramping limits of barter, the Constitution gave Congress power "to coin money, regulate the value thereof, and of foreign coin," together with the functionally related power to "fix the standard of weights and measures." In further assurance that the market should have the uniform and reliable money supply it needed, no state should "coin money; emit bills of credit," or "make anything but gold and silver coin a tender in payment of debts." To enlarge the effective range of trading as well as of other activity, Congress gained power "to establish post offices and post roads." Implicitly accepting as socially desirable the general freedom of individuals to market all goods or services for which they could find customers, the Constitution, "to promote the progress of science and useful arts," authorized Congress to pass laws "securing for limited times to authors and inventors the exclusive right to their respective writings and discoveries." Anticipating issues of policy that would attend overcoming the scarcity of labor in the market, the Constitution empowered Congress "to establish an uniform rule of naturalization." In another provision of tragic implications affecting the labor supply the Constitution also assured that up to 1808 the national government would not interfere with "the migration or importation" of slaves so far as any of the states saw fit to allow. Recognizing the hazards of the market and the need of law to provide orderly and fair dispositions when affairs went badly awry, Congress had power to pass "uniform laws on the subject of bankruptcies throughout the United States." Explicitly preferring some values of free trade, the Constitution declared that "[n]o tax or duty shall be laid on articles exported from any state," and that "[n]o preference shall be given by any regulation of commerce or reve-nue to the ports of one state over those of another; nor shall ves-sels bound to, or from, one state, be obliged to enter, clear, or pay duties in another." Nor might any state, without the consent of Congress, "lay any imposts or duties on imports or exports, except what may be absolutely necessary for executing its in-spection laws," nor lay any "duty of tonnage." Also in implicit favor of affording protection of national law over wide-ranging trade, Article III extended the judicial power of the United States "to all cases of admiralty and maritime jurisdiction" and "to con-troversies . . . between citizens of different states," while Article IV required that "full faith and credit shall be given in each state to the public acts, records, and judicial proceedings of every other state," and that "[t]he citizens of each state shall be entitled to all privileges and immunities of citizens in the several states." In a provision which was to have a large bearing on the develop-ment of private market activity, Article IV also gave Congress "power to dispose of and make all needful rules and regulations respecting the territory or other property belonging to the United States." Finally, in a striking intervention of national law into fields of policy that would ordinarily be the domain of the states, the Constitution forbade any state to pass any "law im-pairing the obligation of contracts"; national interest was impli-cated in assuring that private commitments in market not be upset by state action aimed retroactively at readjusting the terms of bargain arrived at by the transacting parties. Assembled, this catalog is impressive testimony that those who framed and adopted the Constitution accepted the private market as a cen-tral institution in the social order—so central that, without sub-stantial controversy, they wove provisions affecting its care into the structure of government.[2]

True, records of the debates in the Philadelphia convention and in the state ratifying conventions usually contain little to spell out the content of these various constitutional provisions;

this is notably so of the contract clause.[3] Realization of what the Constitution meant for the market waited in large measure on later practice of Congress and on decisions of the Supreme Court. Thus, the reach of commerce clause protection to national free trade against parochial legislation of the states became clear only from the Court's decision in *Gibbons* v. *Ogden* (1824).[4] Nonetheless, the constitutional text provided the necessary base for later developments and in itself bore witness that the policymakers were sensitive to the importance of market concerns.

Contemporary state constitutions contain no comparable elaboration of market-related provisions. But this fact carries no implication that people saw the market as playing less of a role in their lives within the frames of state policy. The relative simplicity of early state constitutions derived from the common assumption that out of the Revolution the state governments directly inherited the policymaking authority theretofore embodied in Parliament, the Crown, and the common law courts; it was the novelty of creating a national government for a federal system that required or invited specifications of market-related policy in the Federal Constitution.[5] From the early nineteenth century the rapid and massive growth of common law doctrine of property and contract serving market needs showed that state courts were quite aware of the large place that the market held in the lives of the people.[6] Though statute law was less prominent, from the first quarter of the nineteenth century state legislation also began to serve working needs of trade, especially to regularize bargaining over land titles.[7]

In the fiscal programs he designed in Washington's first administration, Alexander Hamilton forecast long-term lines of public policy promotive of private economic growth. His analysis offers telling evidence of the central place assigned to the market. Thus, in his *First Report on the Public Credit* (1790) he did not limit his concern to establishing the new national government as a reliable borrower. He argued also that a well-funded national debt "answers most of the purposes of money"; trusted government paper "passes current as specie," so that thereby "trade is extended . . . because there is a larger capital to carry it on," while "[a]griculture and manufactures are also promoted by it, for the like reason that more capital can be commanded to be employed in both, and because the merchant, whose enterprise in foreign trade gives to them activity and extension, has greater means for enterprise."[8] Moreover, to serve what he deemed critical functional needs of the market he accepted sharp political controversy. He provided that the government should pay its outstanding debt at face value, whether the debt be held by original lenders or by speculators who had bought up the evidences of debt at severely depreciated prices. By its terms the old debt was to be paid in full to the first holder or to his assignee. This quality of negotiability was essential to the acceptability and serviceability of government paper for needs of the private market as well as of the government: "[T]he intent in making the security assignable is that the proprietor may be able to make use of his property by selling it for as much as it may be worth in market and that the buyer may be safe in the purchase." Thus the government should unhesitatingly honor the word of its promise to the present holder of its matured debt. To do otherwise would violate the functional integrity of market operations, would be "a breach of contract, a violation of the rights of a fair purchaser." In Hamilton's estimate, to preserve and strengthen the working capacity of the market was worth a major political battle.[9]

In the *Report on the Subject of Manufactures* (1791) Hamilton urged that the national government use its fiscal powers to promote increase of machine-based industrial production through a protective tariff and bounties or subsidies. The market was at the center of his analysis, but in dynamic relation to government's legislative and executive capabilities.

Three elements figured in Hamilton's appraisal. First, he did not accept the private market as a self-sufficient instrument to advance the general welfare. Left to its own motion the market was apt to succumb "to the strong influence of habit and the spirit of imitation; the fear of want of success in untried enterprises; the intrinsic difficulties incident to first essays toward a competition with those who have previously attained to perfection in the business to be attempted; the bounties, premiums, and other artificial encouragements, with which foreign nations second the exertions of their own citizens, in the branches in which they are to be rivaled."[10]

Second, however, Hamilton had no purpose to displace the private market as the principal engine of the economy. He singled out promotion of machine-based industry as a key point for government intervention because experience showed that this was the type of economic activity which promised "prodigious effect," especially in contrast to what he deemed the inherently more static agricultural sector. Implicit was a limiting principle: government should apply its own dynamic only at points or in ways that promised high multiplied results in economic growth.[11]

Third, the ultimate social benefits of his policy would flow from the impacts of expanding private markets characterized by high division of labor, by introduction of new materials and new products, by stimulation of a greater diversity of occupations and outputs, and by challenges which would elicit a wider range of entrepreneurial ambition and skill.

> [T]he results of human exertion may be immensely increased by diversifying its objects. When all the different kinds of industry obtain in a community, each individual can find his proper element and can call into activity the whole vigor of his nature; and the community is benefited by the services of its respective members, in the manner in which each can serve it with most effect. . . . To cherish and stimulate the activity of the human mind, by multiplying the objects of enterprise, is not among the least considerable of the expedients by which the wealth of a nation may be promoted. . . . The spirit of enterprise, useful and prolific as it is, must necessarily be contracted or expanded, in proportion to

the simplicity or variety of the occupations and productions which are to be found in a society. It must be less in a nation of mere cultivators than in a nation of cultivators and merchants; less in a nation of cultivators and merchants than in a nation of cultivators, artificers, and merchants.[12]

Finally, in Hamilton's optimism expanding markets foster social peace. Rather grudgingly Hamilton's *Report* recognized that he must hold out the promise that the bulk of the population who were then in agriculture would gain from promotion of commerce and industry. That promise lay in the growth of purchasing power of those engaged in commerce and industry, which would provide growing markets for the products of the farms.[13] Thus, in his overall analysis, though government was to supply the essential impetus, the broader object was to energize the private market, upon which Hamilton principally relied for vigorous sustained economic growth as well as for social harmony.

The first half of the nineteenth century saw continued expansion of the volume and geographic range of private trade in land, farm produce, manufactured articles, wholesale and retail distribution, and banking and finance.[14] Already by the 1830s Tocqueville was struck by the importance of market dealing in creating the special dynamic of this society: "In democracies nothing is greater or more brilliant than commerce; it attracts the attention of the public and fills the imagination of the multitude; all energetic passions are directed towards it."[15] Not only the well-to-do but also individuals of less means felt the attraction: "Those who live in midst of democratic fluctuations have always before their eyes the image of chance; and they end by liking all undertakings in which chance plays a part. They are therefore all led to engage in commerce, not only for the sake of the profit it holds out to them, but for the love of the constant excitement occasioned by that pursuit."[16]

The early national years provided no more striking evidence of the extent to which people thought and acted in market terms than the readiness with which public policy treated land as a tradeable commodity. Whether among aristocracy, landed gentry, or yeomen, English tradition had regarded landholding as normally fixed in the same owners over long stretches of time. Here, in contrast, land—whether in unsettled areas or in townsites—rapidly became a prime object of private speculative dealing. Farmers railed against absentee speculators who retarded settlement by holding land off the market for future rise in value. But farmers themselves sought profit not simply from cultivating but periodically from selling acres they had opened for tillage.[17] That private holders should enjoy broad capacity to determine the use of the land they occupied and to transfer it was the core policy of the Virginia legislation in which Jefferson took pride. Of like policy were the comparable provisions which became common in state constitutions, abolishing feudal land titles and declaring that all land "be allodial" (that is, owned by individuals independently, free of superior, restrictive claims). Of similar quality were constitutional or statutory provisions limiting long-term agricultural leases and the terms of such leases. Such stipulations meant that private title in fee simple absolute—freehold title—should be the norm of land ownership.[18] There were social and political values embodied in this exaltation of the fee simple; politically influential opinion held that such landholding provided the base of sturdy and responsible roles in society on which a reliable voting population could rest, and fostered in the landowner the self-respect and independence of will that gave his life worth and dignity.[19] But public policy also regarded no aspects of the fee simple title as carrying more meaning for the quality of individual and social life than those by which law recognized in the fee owner broad discretion in using his land for producing marketable values and in deciding when and on what terms to sell it.

In *Fletcher* v. *Peck* (1810) the Supreme Court extended the protection of the contract clause of the Federal Constitution to safeguard a grant of fee simple title in the hands of a bona fide

purchaser against upset by retroactive state legislation.[20] In two
aspects Chief Justice Marshall's opinion indicated that the Court
did not regard the issue as simply that of protecting a vested title
as such. The heart of the matter was protecting the marketable
value of land. First, Marshall emphasized that the original grant
which provided the base for the private title here contested
"when issued, conveyed an estate in fee-simple to the grantee,
clothed with all the solemnities which law can bestow." The critical element was that "[t]his estate was transferrable"—that is,
marketable in law. Second, the present holder had acquired his
title on terms which fit the classic criteria of socially acceptable
market dealing:

> [T]he rights of third persons, who are purchasers without notice
> [of a possible title defect in earlier holders], for a valuable con-
> sideration, cannot be disregarded. Titles which, according to
> every legal test, are perfect are acquired with that confidence
> which is inspired by the opinion that the purchaser is safe. . . . He
> has paid his money for a title good at law; he is innocent, what-
> ever may be the guilt of others, and equity will not subject him to
> the penalties attached to that guilt.[21]

To allow upset of a title so acquired would offend good policy
by impairing socially useful trading in land. The emphasis was
on market traffic: Under a contrary ruling, "[a]ll titles would be
insecure, and the intercourse between man and man would be
very seriously obstructed, if this principle be overturned."[22] Finally, Marshall indicated the deep commitment to the market by
grounding the Court's protection of the bona fide purchaser in
market not only on the contract clause but on a principle of good
social order not dependent on the constitutional text:

> [I]n this case, the estate having passed into the hands of a pur-
> chaser for a valuable consideration, without notice, the state of
> Georgia was restrained, either by general principles which are
> common to our free institutions, or by the particular provisions of
> the Constitution of the United States, from passing a law whereby
> the estate of the plaintiff in the premises so purchased would be

constitutionally and legally impaired and rendered null and void.[23]

At the outset of the new national government, by cessions from the several states which held "western" land claims under Crown grants, the United States became full owner of most of the land under the country's sovereignty west of the Appalachians. The Ordinance of 1785 laid the groundwork for policy governing disposition of this public domain. It established that the norm should be sale by a market procedure—sale at public auction—and sale of fee simple titles. In this restless, mobile society it was politically impracticable for the national government to seek to make itself a perpetual landlord of vast acres suitable for growing crops and forming towns. True, this alternative was not wholly outside the ideas of the times; foreshadowing later public lands legislation, the 1785 ordinance provided for some limited reservations of title in the United States, notably of lands to support schools and of a portion of land bearing valuable minerals. But the narrow specificity of the reservations underlined the dominant policy. The bulk of the public lands should be brought into private ownership under titles favorable to market dealing because unencumbered by lingering claims of government. The ordinance did put a temporary regulatory brake on transfer to private fee simple ownership; land would not be offered to private buyers until completion in any given area of a federal survey establishing a legally defined pattern of boundaries. But there was a market emphasis implicit even in this stipulation. In its immediate impact the requirement of a survey before sale was a restrictive regulation; in a longer view, by standardizing tradeable units of land and tending to reduce costly boundary disputes, the survey provision facilitated market dealing.[24] Despite later variations in program and a good deal of evasion of the ban on settlement before survey, the main lines of national policy continued to hold to the central principle of promoting transfer of land from public to private ownership on terms which made land fully available as marketable goods.[25]

Again the shrewdly observant Tocqueville saw the market orientation of the society made visible—now in the attitudes taken toward land. He was impressed by the extent to which farmland was brought into the main currents of the market because farmers here saw themselves as businessmen and not as peasants:

> Almost all the farmers of the United States combine some trade with agriculture; most of them make agriculture itself a trade. It seldom happens that an American farmer settles for good upon the land which he occupies; especially in the districts of the Far West, he brings land into tillage in order to sell it again, and not to farm it; he builds a farmhouse on the speculation that, as the state of the country will soon be changed by the increase of population, a good price may be obtained for it. . . . Thus the Americans carry their businesslike qualities into agriculture, and their trading passions are displayed in that as in their other pursuits.[26]

From the late nineteenth century no feature of public policy has more clearly shown the hold that the private market has on politically effective opinion than key responses in law to dissatisfactions with the market. Economic growth was accompanied by increasing interlock of modes of producing and distributing goods and services. Technological advances in industry, and opportunities opened by improved transport and communication, fostered large-scale business operations with great concentrations of assets under centralized private direction. These changes produced unprecedented imbalances of bargaining power among farmers, railroads, grain elevators, and banks, between labor and management, and among small firms and big ones. From 1870 on these market imperfections recurrently generated sharp, often highly emotional, sometimes violent economic and political combat. Conceivably these discontents might have surged into active demand that government take over key sectors in which private market dealings stirred deep frustrations. The striking fact is that in these respects the country's politics stayed stubbornly centrist. Those who tried to rally political sentiment to displace the private market orientation of the social system have never achieved material influence. Politically and socially effective opinion has seen the answer to gross market imperfections in public policies intended to make the market work better. Farmers, small business, and consumers generally settled for public utility regulation of railroads and other key facilities, still under private ownership. Small business and as much consumer opinion as showed itself settled for antitrust programs designed to leave the private market in place as a principal resource allocator. Labor settled for legal acceptance and protection of collective bargaining.[27]

Bryce noted that this was a people not given to framing general theories of its social values and their ranking.[28] But implicit in the main currents of public policy were two value judgments which had gained early classic outlines from Jefferson, Madison, and Hamilton, converging on the relations of law and the market. Following Jefferson and Madison, much politically influential opinion distrusted centralized power, public or private, and did not want to see power monopolized by any one sector of society. In later years probably few people knew Jefferson's words, but the sustained practice of politics followed his warning, that "[m]ankind soon learn to make interested use of every right and power which they possess or may assume."[29] Jefferson's prime objection to Hamilton's fiscal policies was that they used government to favor concentrated private financial power, violating proper limits on government and the standard of a market open on fair and equal terms to all bargainers.[30] On the other hand, though Hamilton would use government to overcome the timidity and inertia which he feared would characterize the market left to its own devices, he did not want government to take over the economy. Implicit in his programs was the limiting principle that government should carefully choose its points of intervention. It should act only where its action promised high multiplier returns, measured in such increase of private market activity as would yield "a degree of energy and effect which is not easily conceived."[31] The restraint which characterized late-nineteenth- and early twentieth-century responses to imbalance of power in market showed that prevailing opinion continued to treat a vital private market as an indispensable component of an acceptable structure of social power. This belief embodied some illusion, as well as some sentiment fostered and manipulated by special interests. These limitations do not negate the reality, that market-oriented attitudes had a major effect in shaping the general course of public policy.

THE (QUALIFIED) LEGAL AUTONOMY OF THE MARKET

From the nation's early years large numbers of people who undoubtedly had never heard of Adam Smith acted out his conviction that private market dealings for profit would generally serve common interest as if an invisible hand guided them to that end. By market bargaining they would achieve a workable degree of efficiency in using scarce economic assets. At the same time, they felt, they would reap social and political benefits, in self-respect and entitlement to political participation as useful members of a commonwealth.[32] Theirs was not a dogmatic laissez-faire faith. Hamilton's Federalist party early lost power. But in practice public policy always included substantial readiness to use law in Hamilton's fashion to facilitate the growth of market activity.[33] Nonetheless, public attitudes and public policy put the market about on an equal plane with, if not superior to, government as an institution of social control.[34]

The market did not stand without peril to its existence. Out of the tempering experience of civil strife in England, John Locke warned that individual freedom, including freedom of action in the economy, was exposed to "invasions" by private or public force.[35] England experienced a seventeenth-century middle-class revolt against expansions of Crown prerogative which had overridden the market to serve political ends or the profit of an inner circle of powerholders. The conflict showed that the market needed legal bulwarks to its freedom.[36] Its defenders argued that if the market were to fulfill its public-interest functions, it must enjoy some protected independence to effect efficient allocations of resources according to its own calculus. This function should not be disrupted by intrusion of special privileges imposed by those unwilling to accept the discipline of competitive private bargaining.[37]

This history did not point toward absolute autonomy of market dealings, however. That patron and spokesman of the Anglo-American middle-class tradition, John Locke, framed his concern for rights of private actors in the economy in the context also of concern for needs of the "commonwealth," that is, of the total society of which the private economic sector was only a part. Market autonomy was always a qualified autonomy.[38]

The law of private property and contract embodied law's positive favor for large freedom of private initiative of will in the economy. Locke symbolized this favor for private initiative when he argued that the individual needed no official license to use his own labor productively on opportunities which the natural setting offered and which others had not already preempted by their own labor.[39] In the late eighteenth century Crevecouer praised the openness of this North American society in whch individuals found themselves encouraged to develop their own "schemes" or "designs" for their economic betterment.[40] Contract law gave this approach substance by treating private agreements as presumptively lawful. Judge-made or statute law might firmly and specifically establish a type of bargain as illegal. But otherwise, one who wished to escape fulfilling his promise carried the burden of persuading a court that what the parties had undertaken was in some respect so offensive to good social order that judges should refuse to enforce it.[41] In practice the presumption in favor of the legality of private agreements reflected the norm of dealing; thus the issue of legality became material in only 2 of approximately 700 forest-products contract cases that reached the Wisconsin Supreme Court over the span of the state's long involvement with that industry.[42] Practice here in this respect fulfilled the often cited summary of policy in an English decision of 1875:

> It must not be forgotten that you are not to extend arbitrarily those rules which say that a given contract is void as being against public policy, because if there is one thing which more than another public policy requires it is that men of full age and competent understanding shall have the utmost liberty of contracting, and that their contracts when entered into freely and voluntarily shall be held sacred and shall be enforced by Courts of justice. Therefore, you have this paramount public policy to consider—that you are not lightly to interfere with this freedom of contract.[43]

From about mid-nineteenth century the doctrine that normally individuals need no official license to become actors in market took on an extension that proved of great import for the future structure of the economy and general patterns of political and social power. Judges and then legislators applied the presumption favoring private initiative of will not only to individual but also to group action.

In *Commonwealth* v. *Hunt* (1842) Chief Justice Shaw declared for the Massachusetts Supreme Judicial Court that the state had the burden of proving that a private association for profit was a criminal conspiracy, either because it pursued a wrongful purpose or used wrongful means; private association in market was presumptively lawful.[44] Immediately at issue was the activity of a trade union seeking a closed shop. From a court otherwise favorable to entrepreneurial values, the decision attested the high value put on private initiative generally; indeed, Shaw's analysis showed awareness of its helpful implications for broader market dealing.[45]

The course of legislative practice was less straightforward than Shaw's decision but no less firm in outcome. In less than a generation—between 1850 and 1880—state legislatures departed from an older tradition that granted corporate charters only jealously and sparingly, and churned out special acts of incorporation by the hundreds, in what became quite standard patterns. In the late nineteenth century, states supplanted special chartering with general incorporation acts. Under the general acts, as these developed by the early twentieth century, entrepreneurs could obtain incorporation through a routinized administrative process, on terms left largely to be determined by choice of the promoters. Thus, in substance statutory policy matched Shaw's common law doctrine: the presumption of public policy favored broad freedom for private initiative in organizing associated effort for market activity.[46]

In its own fashion the growth of a body of public utility law through the nineteenth and into the early twentieth century evidenced the strength of the Lockean presumption against requiring official licenses for private contract dealing. That branch of policy bore mainly on adjusting the market to the general social context. The point relevant here is that, up to the 1930s, received doctrine was that legal regulation of prices and quality of service offered by firms was exceptional, warranted only by the community's peculiar dependence on certain lines of business. In that view it was a matter of high substantive importance that public utility law was a specialized area. It did not represent the norm; the norm was that entry into and continuance in market did not depend on official license.[47]

As with contracts, so public policy regarding land title and land use offered broad scope for private will in allocating resources. In the absence of particular statutory regulations, the law dealing with private injuries (tort law) developed a counterpart of the presumption favoring free contract. A lawful possessor might normally decide on using land in ways profitable to him; the burden of persuasion lay on a public prosecutor or a private complainant to establish that the possessor's use carried such socially harmful aspects that a court should rule it a public or private nuisance.[48] Policy regarding land title showed a similar pattern but—in a manner analogous to that taken by the statute law of business corporations—developed through a more involved course of affairs. By Locke's principles anyone should by his labor become entitled to claim the law's protection for his control of land not already productively occupied by another's labor. In limited degree common law resembled Locke in recognizing title acquired by adverse possession or prescriptive use.[49] In this country, however, the norm of policy required positive action by law to found land titles. The legal factor that dominated the course of title west of the Appalachians was the original ownership of most of the land by the United States. In that setting most private ownership in the expanding country had to begin under official grant or license. However, Congress adopted a central policy not far from Locke's principles; so long as the public lands proved suited to agriculture, the norm was to transfer them to private holders in fee simple for low cash prices or in exchange for the labor of opening them to cultivation.[50] This policy was so taken for granted that, without controversy or felt need for reexamination, it was applied in original dispositions of the Lake States forest lands, which were not suited to farming. Once cut for their most valuable timber, these acres were usually allowed to revert to the government for unpaid taxes. Thus, the practical though uncalculated outcome was as if the United States had leased or licensed the land for logging without any of the stipulations a prudent lessor might fix to preserve the long-term productivity of the forest. Carried along by inertia as well as by the immediate pressures of the lumber market, this history attested the momentum of official and popular favor for giving large rein to private will in using land.[51] The United States became a long-term landlord only when settlement reached the semi-arid West. In the second half of the twentieth century the old lines of policy again came to the fore, in protests of grazing, mining, and timber interests in western states against such limits as the United States imposed when it licensed private use of the public domain.[52]

The qualified autonomy of the private market rested on important negative as well as positive contributions of law. Criminal law and the law of civil wrongs (torts) offered some deterrents and redress for private invasions of market bargaining by force or fraud. Often tardily and unevenly, lawmakers extended these bulwarks of market processes as markets extended and their modes of operation became more elaborate, and as wrongdoers became more sophisticated. Thus, legislatures enlarged criminal sanctions to deal with embezzlement as well as with theft, with fraud in obtaining money or credit or insurance, and with theft of electric power or industrial secrets.[53] On the civil side statute law sought through administrative process to prevent fraud in offering or trading corporate securities, first by state "blue sky" laws and later by the body of legislation administered by the federal Securities and Exchange Commission and filled out further by accretion of federal court precedent. Analogous legislation regulated commodities trading. After weak beginnings in the nineteenth century, twentieth-century state and federal legislation expanded protections of the pocketbooks and health and safety of consumers against deceptive or recklessly dangerous marketing practices.[54] The expanding array of criminal and civil provisions against disruption of the market calculus by private aggression or greed highlighted a basic reality. The market—an institution which presupposes peaceful, rational, and mutually acceptable exchanges by bargain—could exist only within a frame of social order. The values at stake were at base relatively elementary and simple. Yet to implement them in increasingly large and complex arenas of dealing demanded more intense, sustained, and sophisticated legal effort than lawmakers usually furnished. An enduring characteristic of the legal order was that legislatures were much readier to declare substantive policy than to provide adequately to make it work.[55]

To perform the efficiency function by which common opinion legitimized the market, the market needed protection not only against private invasion but also against abuses of public power.

Locke pointed to this aspect of legal bulwarks of market processes when he justified the middle-class revolution which displaced royal prerogative expanded under the Stuarts. Protected autonomy for the market was deeply implicated in Locke's prescriptions for the supremacy of an elected assembly as a prime lawmaker. In this context, Locke summarized four "bounds which the trust that is put in them by the society, and the law of God and Nature, have set to the legislative power of every commonwealth, in all forms of government." Though they were capable of supporting other values also, his four limiting principles spelled independence for the private market, making it free of legal interventions moved by private or narrowly political advantage. (1) He put first a criterion of equal protection, "to govern by promulgated established laws, not to be varied in particular cases, but to have one rule for rich and poor, for the favorite at court and the countryman at plough." His standard was not without ambiguity: Did it apply to the substance of statute law or only to equality in its application? In the context of the times, however, the reference to court favorites pointedly implied protection of free market dealing against competitive advantage conferred simply by force of law. (2) He declared what in the late nineteenth century the United States Supreme Court would define as the standard of substantive due process of law under the Fourteenth Amendment: that public power should be used for public good and not simply for private gain. ("[T]hese laws also ought to be designed for no other end ultimately but the good of the people.") (3) The power to "raise taxes on the property of the people" must lie only in the consent of the people, given directly or through their elected legislature. (4) Finally, the legislature must not "transfer the power of making laws to anyone else, or place it anywhere but where the people have." The third and fourth propositions particularly reflect distrust of the potentials for executive abuse of public power affecting resource allocations, given past Crown grants of trade monopolies.[56]

The general context of Locke's analysis of constitutional principles shows that his prime focus was on rights of individuals, though his discussion of religious toleration included assertion of freedom of association.[57] He did not foresee that the business corporation would become the most important form of private enterprise. But when the corporation came on the scene in the United States, the Supreme Court early began to treat it as entitled to legal protection of its freedom in the market on terms analogous to those accorded individuals. The Marshall Court broke this ground by extending to corporate charters the safeguard which the contract clause of the national Constitution provided against retroactive change of charter terms by state statute.[58] In the first part of the nineteenth century the Court took care to preserve the authority of states to set conditions on entry into local markets of corporations chartered by other states. But it tempered this position by a readiness to find that, as a matter of comity, a state would be presumed to allow entry of an outside corporation to do local business if it had not explicitly raised barriers.[59] Under the Fourteenth Amendment the Court greatly expanded constitutional guarantees of market autonomy when it ruled that corporations were "persons" within the protections of the standards of due process and equal protection of the laws.[60]

Law in the nineteenth century reflected a continued concern that discriminatory uses of executive power at state and local levels threatened fair operation of market processes. Taxation was a policy area which received notably sustained attention, with an emphasis akin to Locke's array of constitutional principles. As developed by the Supreme Court, the due process clauses of the Fifth and Fourteenth Amendments sanctioned judicial review of the fairness of tax collection procedures; further, in the equal protection clause of the Fourteenth Amendment the Court found ample authority for judges to upset discriminatory tax assessments.[61] Tax laws became increasingly complicated and technical, especially with the advent of the income tax. Taxpayers thus found wider opportunities to challenge tax levies not only on constitutional grounds but also on charges that they violated statutory standards.[62] There is reason to question how far these formal protections worked to protect the market against abuse of the tax system for private or political advantage. Especially in the nineteenth century, public administration had few professionals and operated with ill-trained staff most often apponted under political patronage. Lawsuits were expensive in money and in delay. With more confidence, however, we can attribute market protection to one particular development. A common abuse of general property taxes under state law was the tendency of local assessors to favor their home areas by undervaluing taxable property, hoping that the greater burden would fall on other local units. Consequently, from the late nineteenth century state legislatures began to create central control boards to equalize assessments over the whole taxing sovereignty. At first only advisory, these central agencies finally gained authority to require adjustment of local valuations to meet fair statewide standards.[63]

Legislation, as well as executive or administrative action, could produce tax discrimination hostile to fair market operations. Here, too, constitutional principle stood for market protection; the problems were those of implementing principle. By the late nineteenth century state constitutions commonly declared Locke's equal protection standard with specific reference to taxation, by declaring, as did the Wisconsin Constitution in 1848, that "[t]he rule of taxation shall be uniform."[64] Later the United States Supreme Court enlarged the concept of equal protection under the Fifth and Fourteenth Amendments to embrace the substance and not merely the application of tax laws.[65]

National revenue laws provided the most notorious examples of special interest maneuver. Before the Sixteenth Amendment finally validated federal income taxation, the tariff offered a fertile field for private advantage at the expense of free competition in international markets affecting the United States. In practice more than in declared doctrine the Supreme Court applied a strong presumption of constitutionality on behalf of the protective tariff. Judicial review thus never curbed invasions of market autonomy in this area of policy. The presumption was bulwarked by the Court's related doctrine, that if a tariff act appeared reasonably calculated to yield revenue, the Court would not upset it because other motives might have figured in its passage.[66] So far as market autonomy got any backing in the tariff area it did so mainly from the wholly pragmatic competition of lobbies before Congress. From time to time the Democratic party made free trade a rallying cry. The 1930s depression highlighted the damaging impact of protectionist trade wars among the nations and for a time fostered some agreement on limiting special-interest domination of tariff policy. Prime symbols of this turn of policy were reciprocal trade treaties negotiated in the New Deal years and, after World War II, the country's participation in the General Agreement on Trade and Tariffs. But in the late twentieth century this has been a field of shifting alignments as special interests continue to press for advantages that do not square with the rationale of free markets.[67]

Through a century of tariff-making, distributions of special-interest favors ranged so broadly that tariff policy was highly resistant to claims on behalf of market autonomy. An analogous pattern marked development of internal revenue policy as the federal income tax made increasing claims on the economy. Special-interest advantages proliferated to a point near to scandal in the complex, technical intricacies of income tax legislation and the maze of administrative regulations and precedents that developed under the statutes.[68] Experience with the tariff and the income tax showed that political inertia gave great leverage to determined, sharply focused interests, as they confronted diffuse bodies of general taxpayers and consumers. As with the tariff, so with the income tax a strong presumption of constitutionality protected Congress from any material curb by the Supreme Court.[69] Enough controversy continued over tax favors for private interests to keep alive the promarket, Lockean principles of equal protection and care for general interest. But these principles were regularly on the defensive.

Profit-seeking interests did not confine to tax laws their search for market advantages. The first major area of contest on this score involved grants of statutory charters to business corporations. Before 1880 most charters existed under special acts of legislation. Their special character made these objects of egalitarian objection and suspicion through an early generation of political polemic.[70] However, as the corporate form became common in the business world, most special charters outside the unusual area of public utilities showed little evidence of special privilege. What most businessmen wanted from incorporation were utilitarian features which posed no offense to Lockean principles so long as access to standard forms of incorporation was readily available to all who asked. From the late nineteenth century on, states substituted general incorporation acts for special charters. In mid-twentieth century the then standard pattern of general incorporation acts became so favorable to prerogatives of entrepreneurs as to raise new policy issues concerning investors and the general public. But these were issues of breadth; they did not raise problems of discrimination among particular dealers in the market.[71]

As private market activity grew in variety, range, and impact from the 1880s on, so did legal regulations of market dealing. Typically lawmakers declared that they acted to protect the market's integrity against fraud or restraint of trade, or to protect nonmarket interests in public health, safety, or morals. But lobbyists could seek regulation as a weapon in business competition. Statutes could handicap those regulated as against competitors who were free of the specially tailored restrictions, or could offer to those already established protective shields against newcomers to market. Thus, for a time dairy industry lobbies scored legislative coups by obtaining laws which banned or hampered sale of oleomargarine.[72] In the twentieth century, in the name of fair trade and consumer protection, legislatures have multiplied the number of occupations entry to which require a license from an official body, sometimes a body selected from the ranks of those already in the business.[73] The play of special interests has not been as overt in these fields of "police power" regulation as in the area of taxation. But it has been sufficient to make substantial inroads on the "bounds" of concern for equality and public interest which Locke had declared in defining "the trust" the society put in the legislative power.

The chief executive's veto power has provided some internal check. Deriving office from a broader electorate than do individual legislators, a state governor may feel freer to veto a bill which he finds to be only a special-interest favor to particular competitors in market.[74] The president has the broadest voter base of all. Thus, President Eisenhower provided a sharp reminder of the chief executive's power to nullify otherwise effective special-interest pressure. In 1956 he vetoed a bill to remove legal curbs on pricing natural gas because he felt that the industry had engaged in grossly improper lobbying practices.[75] However, the veto power has not come into play often on the state or the national scene.

Enforcing due process and equal protection standards embodied in the Fifth and Fourteenth Amendments or in counterpart provisions of state constitutions, the courts offer a possible external check on legislation that yields to narrowly focused lobbies. Yet, judges normally have given economic regulatory legislation the full benefit of a presumption of constitutionality. The Supreme Court states the presumption in terms that make rebuttal difficult. The challenger must convince the Court that the legislators could have found no reasonable basis in public interest for what they did. If the legislature might reasonably find two or more public-interest justifications for a statute affecting market behavior, the challenger must rebut each justification, else the statute will stand. So long as the Court applies protective doctrine of this sweep, it will usually not be hard for ingenious

supporters to tender reasonable hypotheses in support of a challenged regulation beyond what a challenger can upset. It was
symbolic that the early classic case invoking the presumption
used it to sustain a Pennsylvania statute which banned sale of
oleomargarine, for the declared purposes of protecting public
health and preventing fraud on consumers.[76] The Court there
suggested an opening to readier rebuttal of the presumption, if
the challenger could show that the statute was enacted only
under "pretense" of serving the declared public purposes. The in-
timation was that if an improper purpose were mingled with a
proper one, the mingling of bad with good might be enough to
invalidate the statute. But the Court did not thereafter develop
this approach through analysis of legislative "motive" as an effective base for curbing successes of special-interest lobbies. At
length the main current of Court doctrine has rejected as an improper extension of judicial review inquiry into legislative
motive in challenges to the validity of legislation relevant
primarily to market regulation.[77] As with tax laws, so in wider
fields of economic regulation the competition of interest groups
within the legislative arena provides the principal means of enforcing Locke's canon favoring market autonomy against favors
conferred by law.[78]

LAW'S CONTRIBUTIONS TO EXTENSION
OF THE MARKET

Property law and contract law have been central elements but
not the only legal elements that have contributed to the existence
and operation of the market. Three other areas of public policy,
if not indispensable, have been material in promoting the great
scale and pervasive reach which market activity has achieved in
the United States. These expansive influences have derived from
(1) legal provisions affecting the supply of money, (2) federalism, and (3) the availability of the corporate form for business

enterprise. Scale and reach have been important not simply for the constitution of the market itself, but also for its impact on other sectors of the society—on the condition of the society's resource base, its politics, its pattern of social status, and the values toward which its people oriented their lives. The next chapter considers some of those broader implications of the extended influence of market activities; here the focus is on the character of the market itself.

The Law of Property and Contract in Support of Transactions

Legal security of private titles and legal freedom of private contract have been central in the considerable autonomy the private market has enjoyed relative to government. These legal guarantees also encouraged private dealers to develop volume, continuity, and stability in market transactions. Law did not make markets, however; business practice made markets. Thus, there is ground for questioning law's importance. To what extent have titles been stable, to what extent have people performed their contracts, because they feared law's sanctions? There is evidence that the observable regularities of market behavior derive mainly from causes outside the law. People respect titles and fulfill contracts in most instances because they perceive that it is in their interest to do so. One who would trade in the future must not get a reputation for repudiating his deals. Where parties have profited from a continuing business relation, their experience puts a premium on not disturbing that relation by failing to perform their agreements. Custom, habit, and the desire for the approval of peers may also support grants and promises. The law of property and contract has had long, involved histories of doctrinal development. But the growth of these stores of doctrine does not in itself prove that they were major facts in maintaining the vitality of the market. Beyond the doctrinal record, in estimating law's roles we must depend largely on circumstantial evidence and on patterns of behavior we know through our own experience which seem likely to have had counterparts in earlier times.[79]

Property law contributes to market activity by defining tradeable items which law will recognize as subjects of bargaining. Thus, federal and state land grants provided bases for the bulk of land titles dealt in west of the Appalachians. The federal land survey helped mark out reliably identifiable tracts for market exchange; in its time the public survey standardized bargainable items in land as later the law of corporation finance has legitimized standard units of trade in stocks and bonds on the exchanges.[80] Property and contract law have linked to promote dealing in less tangible items of value. Woodsmen cruised the forest, making notes of the likely lumber yield of timberlands. They could sell their notes to investors in part because law contributed to the marketable value of the cruiser's notes by supporting his claim to exclude others from the benefit of his gathered knowledge unless they paid for it.[81] Property law has fostered market ventures by assuring that one who exchanges his money for land or goods can expect the seller's commitment to stand; a granted title carries the grantor's legally firm undertaking not to disturb the transfer.[82] People have given deeds, recorded titles, furnished abstracts of title, bought title insurance, entered into finely drawn bond indentures, and issued or obtained equipment trust receipts, warehouse receipts, and trust receipts. The variety and bulk of actions thus taken in legal form to assure the validity and security of titles are persuasive circumstantial evidence that people have organized much market activity in reliance on law.[83] Their reliance has been most marked where they loan or advance money and want security; in this domain, at least, their activities have shown that they act with sober attention to the legal consequences of possible breakdowns in relations.[84]

The contributions of contract law to market operations have been less formally defined. The domain of contract has been most distinct from that of property where bargains require some time and continuing or postponed action for their consummation. Most such agreements have been performed to the practical satisfaction of the parties. The growth of market activity has evidenced that this is so; market volume could not have developed as it did if transactions could typically have been carried through only under pressure of the slow, costly, uncertain, and limited remedies available in contract law. Viewed in this light, contract law has figured in affairs in two different ways. It has facilitated initiation of transactions. And it has dealt with salvage after major breakdowns in relationships.

Contract law has helped promote market activity in two fashions. The policy favoring freedom of contract has limited official interference with private will. But it has also encouraged private transactions by presuming their legality.[85] Contract law has had another promotional influence by helping develop standardized forms of dealing. Standardization has economized effort in contriving deals; it has built confidence by providing predictable incidents of bargains where the parties have not spelled out particular details; it has helped extend the range of trafficking by offering more secure bases for exchange among parties not otherwise in close, continuing contact. Again, however, there has been a mix of legal and other than legal influences. In the first instance law has been more likely to follow than to lead business ambitions and practices, though with time customs and conventions of lawmakers and lawyers have tended to impose the law's own institutional constraints on business practice.[86] As Mansfield drew on merchants' customs in giving law's sanction to the idea of negotiability, so later in the United States the credit needs of farmers, merchants, and business promoters pressed lawyers to devise terms on which loans might be secured by a lien on growing crops, on shifting stocks of goods, or on land or operating equipment acquired by the debtor after he had executed a bond indenture.[87] Granted that businessmen usually have been the prime initiators, nonetheless lawyers and judges have contributed the developed forms of security on which a credit economy was built. In the twentieth century the common designation of "boilerplate" to characterize standard provisions in extended-term agreements witnesses how far the law's contributions have entered into everyday practice. By this time, too, reliance on legal standardization has become marked in the mix of public regulation and private contrivance governing customers' relations with public utilities—in standard bills of lading or warehouse receipts, insurance contracts, or agreements to provide electric power. Collective bargaining contracts then have provided another large field of increasingly standardized terms of dealing. There is reason to question how far the threat of legal sanctions has led people to carry out their agreements. But we should not overlook the ways in which law helped bring agreements into being.[88]

However we appraise its influence on the market, contract litigation has been a continuing part of the business of lawyers and courts. Even in the relatively simple circumstances of the Wisconsin lumber industry between 1836 and 1915, 783 actions on contracts reached the Wisconsin Supreme Court; a substantial additional number of such suits undoubtedly ended in trial courts.[89] In the twentieth century suits on contracts may have tended to form a smaller proportion of court business; increases in personal injury suits and in family law problems have appeared to compete more heavily for judges' time. Even so, such shifts do not prove that twentieth-century courts handle markedly smaller percentages of all controversies over contracts than they had earlier; without inventories of total disputes experienced in the course of market activity, the matter defies measurement.[90]

Both in the nineteenth and twentieth centuries most contract litigation seems to have been between middle-class suitors, most often involving entrepreneurs of modest scale. Until twentieth-century installment selling brought many business creditors into small claims courts as plaintiffs, suits involving workers or consumers did not loom large. In the nineteeth and twentieth centuries alike the largest firms have rarely appeared as plaintiffs or as defendants in suits between business peers. Where litigation has arisen between big firms, it has usually been resolved by out-of-court settlement. Otherwise, big companies usually have appeared only as defendants in consumer suits for defective goods.[91] Such patterns in contract litigation offer further circumstantial evidence that ordinarily calculations of business interest have been more influential than concern for possible legal liability in determining performance of bargains.

Yet, despite costs in time, effort, and money, there has been sufficient volume of contract litigation to indicate that the availability of legal processes plays a role in market behavior once relationships break down. Contract law and the costs of contract lawsuits provide bargaining counters affecting the likelihood and terms of settlements. Further, contract law provides some ultimate means for picking up the pieces or mopping up after affairs have gone badly awry.[92] When this has happened, there have been needs which law could help meet. Law has provided procedures to realize such assets as might be salvaged and to determine who got them. Law has put limits on what otherwise might be liabilities so heavy as to destroy parties' ability ever to return to the market. An outstanding example of such salvage uses of law has been the development of procedures for corporate reorganization under shelter of court orders. As great enterprises played increasingly important roles in the economy, the possibility of their total collapse carried unacceptable consequences for the economy. In the nineteenth century financial problems of trunk-line railroads posed prime instances of this threat to market stability. Investment bankers and lawyers had adapted the real estate mortgage to financing the roads. In this setting, a default by the debtor might seem to pose only familiar issues of foreclosing a mortgage and winding up the enterprise. But the community could not suffer loss of its rail service; simple distribution of net assets on a final dissolution was not socially practicable. Moreover, it would not satisfy the interests of those contending for future management of railroad networks. Over some two generations public and private interests slowly and painfully combined to develop a new body of law of corporate reorganization under which prime goals were not only to give some protection to secured creditors, but also to give new life to enterprises needed or useful to serve the community. By the 1930s a pattern of policy which at first unfolded through an uncertain body of case law to deal with special problems of railroads became available to business generally, under federal bankruptcy legislation.[93]

The Money Supply

Market dealing could attain no great scale if it had to proceed by barter. Private business practice could develop acceptable tokens of exchange; receipts of London goldsmiths once provided an early type of specie-secured currency. But experience early showed the utility of legal measures to furnish coin and currency produced by official agencies or by private sources under government regulation. The framers attested this experience by granting the national government authority to coin money and—as the Supreme Court later ruled—to issue paper currency or to delegate that function to nationally chartered banks.[94] The practical importance of assured standardization of money tokens was underlined by the strict limitations the national Constitution put on the states, forbidding them to issue their own currency (bills of credit) or to make any commodity other than gold or silver legal tender. The Supreme Court qualified the rigor of the constitutional ban, but the substance of the limitation stood; states never became direct major sources of currency.[95] Yet, through most of the nineteenth century and into the first half of the twentieth, public policy did not serve the market well in provisions for a money supply. Two developments greatly expanded the money stock to match expanding markets, but both developments were sadly lacking in discipline. The Supreme Court declared that the Constitution's ban on state bills of credit did not forbid issue of circulating notes by state-chartered, private banks.[96] These issues grew fast between 1830 and 1860, but under no uniform or reliable policing of their quality or quantity relative to the needs of trade.[97] The same period saw increased use of checks drawn on bank deposits largely created by bank loans; by the second half of the nineteenth century deposit-check money representing bank credit provided the bulk of the working money supply.[98] Under Nicholas Biddle from about 1824 to 1832 the Second Bank of the United States imposed some salutary central planning and discipline on the money supply, including the supply of bank credit. The lesson seemed clear—that a national monopoly of coinage and of government-issued currency sanctioned by the national Constitution should be extended to embrace all elements of the money stock.[99] But the time was not ready. Powerful political opinion distrusted a strong, positive role for the national government in the economy; thus, when the nation's financial need in the Civil War required some action, the creation of a new pattern of nationally incorporated banks followed the model, not of centralized authority such as Biddle's bank had wielded, but rather of the open-market style of state policy under which an indefinite number of private entrepreneurs might obtain national charters. This measure was accompanied by direct issue of notes of the national government but without provision for managing the issues relative to the changing course of the economy. Congress did assert a national monopoly to the extent of imposing a prohibitive federal tax which ended issues of circulating notes by state-chartered banks, and the Supreme Court sustained the measure. But this action did not bar provision of credit (and hence of deposit-check money) by state banks, and bank credit already constituted the bulk of the money supply.[100] Not until Congress created the Federal Reserve System in 1913 did public policy move toward sustained, central discipline of the money supply. Even then in practice it was not until the 1950s that the Federal Reserve management learned how to use its authority to buy and sell government securities in ways which have provided it a flexible process for affecting the general course of bank credit.[101]

Law can disserve as well as serve the market, and in the matter of a money supply most of the time it has rendered much disservice.[102] The most dramatic witness to the costs of inadequate monetary policy was a succession of periods of boom and bust, punctuated with financial panic. Factors other than the state of the money supply contributed to ups and downs in the general course of business. But defects of the money system figured heavily in events and sometimes precipitated disaster.[103] Various factors entered into failures to provide adequate governance of the money supply. In the forepart of the nineteenth century there was lively distrust of national power. A related but also in part an independent element was the want of administrative experience and skill in national and in state government. These lacks were compounded by the limits of economic theory and knowledge, notably, until well into the twentieth century, the want of sufficient, reliable statistical data on the general course of business. Indeed, even after the Federal Reserve began bolder management of money at mid-twentieth century, its often fumbling performance has shown that want of theory and knowledge continue to limit its capacity.[104] However, values and ways of thinking bred by the market itself have had much to do with the tardy and uncertain growth of monetary policy. Market-bred traditions have favored broadly dispersed, rather than centralized, decisionmaking. So, too, market-bred attitudes have distrusted elected officials, seen as likely to seek votes by using controls on money supply to redistribute wealth and income in violation of the market's proper degree of autonomy. The concerns which put into the Federal Constitution the contract clause and the ban on state bills of credit have had their counterparts in the nineteenth- and twentieth-century interest groups solicitous for the market.[105]

Federalism

Markets in the United States have grown to span broad sections of the country and even to embrace the nation. Factors other than public policy have figured in this growth. In the nineteenth century the great expanse of tillable lands and the availability of natural assets in minerals, timber, waterways, and waterpower attracted entrepreneurial energy. From the 1880s on, but especially in the twentieth century, headlong developments in the technology of production and distribution and in entrepreneurial and managerial skill have generated outputs on a scale which only markets of sectional or national scope could accommodate.[106] Granted the importance of such influences outside legal processes, nonetheless the country's political arrangements have been critical to realizing a national free trade area; the difficult efforts of twentieth-century Europe to achieve an analogous common market throw into sharp relief the accomplishment in the United States.[107]

In a variety of provisions the Federal Constitution sought to promote national free trade and to protect it against parochial pressures.[108] Concern for social peace as well as for economic growth entered into this national emphasis; Balkanized trade policies could threaten domestic tranquillity, as did the South Carolina nullification threat in the 1830s. But the high value which people put on the vitality of extended markets was also a prime moving factor. So Madison praised the scope which a federal system would give against threats of particularized economic interest. Of like import was Hamilton's *Report on the Subject of Manufactures* as it forecast the constructive interdependence of markets for agriculture and for the products of industry.[109]

The Supreme Court has been the central agency which earliest and most often has acted to implement constitutional policy favoring national markets. The Court has most readily exercised authority by negative rather than by affirmative action; hence, it has been the prime agency to enforce the contract clause and the limits which the Constitution put on direct action by states to affect the money supply. But the record included a striking exception to the Court's veto role affecting money, when the Court ruled that banknotes issued by private, state-chartered banks did not offend the ban on state bills of credit. The decision fit historical reality; the ban on bills of credit originated long before anyone conceived that states would charter hundreds of note-issuing banks. Yet, the court might have ruled plausibly that such banknotes violated the substance of the constitutional prohibition which derived from fear that state policy would yield to debtors' pressures to inflate the currency. The Court chose not to take that road because it recognized that even by the 1830s the growing national economy was so dependent for its operations on the swelling volume of circulating bank notes that to hold against their validity would seriously disturb the working capacity of the market.[110]

The Court's boldest action to protect national free trade was taken under the commerce clause. In that grant of power to Congress it found an implied, judicially enforcible negative on state legislation which explicitly or in likely effect discriminated against interstate commerce, or which put legal or practical burdens on such commerce to a degree unwarranted by proper state interest. By their allocation of the burden of persuasion the justices have underlined the strength of the policy, thus favoring national free trade. Their doctrine—if not always their practice—has generally accorded a presumption of constitutionality to state laws regulating marketplace behavior. But if the challenger of a state statute makes a *prima facie* case of discrimination against interstate commerce, the Court has put on the supporter of the statute a heavy burden of justifying it as serving a legitimate public interest; indeed, if the statute is in its terms discriminatory, the decisions have amounted to holding it unconstitutional on its face. Where the issue has been whether the act put a nondiscriminatory but undue burden on doing interstate business, the ordinary presumption of constitutionality has generally applied. But if a particular state regulation departs sharply from types of laws commonly found among the states, late-twentieth-century decisions have treated the uniqueness of the burden as requiring that the statute's supporter show strong justification for it.[111] Through the nineteenth and into the late twentieth century a good many lawsuits have thus invoked the authority of federal courts to enforce the implied limits which the commerce clause put on state concessions to local economic interests. Continuing invocation of the commerce clause is persuasive evidence that in this domain national law has made a material contribution to freedom of broad markets.[112]

Potentially, the commerce clause granted Congress generous power to impose its own limits or vetoes on state laws that it found to encroach on national free trade, or to provide its own positive encouragement to markets that reached over state lines. That this power lay in Congress may have encouraged the Court to bolder use of the reviewing authority it asserted under the commerce clause alone; if the Court misread the proper balance of interests between national and state policymaking, Congress could substitute its own assessment.[113] But well into the twentieth century Congress had made only limited use of its power to these ends. The Court found in two acts of Congress federal protection of interstate navigation and of interstate telegraph business.[114] After the court had pointed the way by invalidating state regulation of interstate railroad rates, Congress slowly and haltingly undertook to set national terms for providing transport facilities essential to national markets.[115]

In other respects, also, congressional action on behalf of broad markets was slow and uneven; substantial development of Congress's role came only well into the twentieth century. Not until 1898 did Congress make sustained use of its power to adopt uniform bankruptcy laws. For the first two generations of big business in the United States, public policy dealt with financial embarrassments of big corporations—especially the railroads—only through a costly and often uncertain and unfair patchwork of judge-made law centering on the equity receivership. Only in the 1930s did Congress use its bankruptcy power to provide comprehensive, more fairly balanced procedures for corporate reorganization.[116] Hamilton had forecast vigorous use of the taxing and spending powers of Congress to set and implement priorities in allocating capital among different sectors of the national economy.[117] Congress used its power to dispose of public lands in ways analogous to Hamilton's ideas when it fostered growth of commercial agriculture and subsidized railroad construction, but it did so piecemeal.[118] It enacted protective tariffs more often as products of opportunistic coalitions of special interests than of the planned development which Hamilton had envisaged.[119] The Sixteenth Amendment, authorizing Congress to create an income tax, armed the national government with greater means than it had before had to use fiscal power to stabilize markets. The New Deal made faltering experiments with this role.[120] Later, the Employment Act of 1946 explicitly legitimized use of government's powers over money and the public purse to moderate swings of business, though in a framework of policy much diluted by bargained compromises among contending interest groups.[121] Not until the second half of the twentieth century did lawmakers seriously consider adjusting tax law to help cope with social costs of deflation and inflation.[122] In 1933, in an exceptional stroke of economic planning, the national government drew on its spending and commerce powers to create the Tennessee Valley Authority. Thus it provided a Hamilton-style, subsidized base for expanding private markets across an entire economically undeveloped region.[123]

However, the TVA program has not represented the main currents of policy. The Constitution endowed the national government with broad authority to foster and protect private markets of sectional or national scope. Chiefly through the Supreme

Court the central government has furnished substantial negative protection to national free trade by striking down responses which state legislatures have made to parochial interests. Compared with the more flexible responses possible through lawsuits fueled by complaints of specially aggrieved interests, Congress has been a ponderous machinery to put in action against particular encroachments of state law on national free trade. True, Congress has the potential which the Courts do not for positive action to encourage broad market activity. Congress did enough to make national legislative, executive, and administrative action material factors affecting the constitution of national markets. But Congress's performance has also often been tardy, hesitant, and incomplete; the record has reflected its always close dependence on local electorates. Congress has found it easier to represent narrower than broader interests, and easier to follow tradition or inertia in favor of old practices of limited markets or in favor of old roles of state law than to innovate positively on behalf of markets of national reach and vigor. Federalism has been a major influence on the character of the market, but the federal system carries no built-in guaranty of effectiveness.

Corporations

After 1820 public policy was increasingly ready to make the corporate form of organization available to business. From about 1750 to 1820 legislatures granted special corporate charters sparingly to profit-seeking enterprises, most of them a type later times would call public utilities. Between 1830 and the 1870s most business corporation charters were created by special acts of legislation, but legislatures came to grant them almost routinely, and mostly on terms which became quite routinized. In the meantime legislatures began to enact general incorporation acts on standard terms, available as an option to seeking special charters; the earliest general acts were for philanthropic organizations, but soon there were general acts also for business enterprises. After 1870, often by constitutional provision, the states began to end special chartering, required that in-corporators resort to the general acts, and included in the general statutes some regulatory terms protective of investors and creditors. At the end of the nineteenth century New Jersey and Delaware pioneered in what became the norm of twentieth-century general corporation statutes, dropping older regulatory provisions and on the whole allowing promoters of an enterprise substantial freedom to set their own terms of organization; now the prime emphasis tended to be not on protecting investors or creditors but on giving large scope to entrepreneurial energy. From the 1930s, state and then federal statutory regulation of corporate business developed mostly outside the frame of corporation law proper, through such legislation as that on corporation finance (state "blue sky" laws and the federal laws centered on the SEC), on labor relations (centered on the National Labor Relations Act and its amendments), on occupational health and safety (centered earlier in state workers' compensation and industrial acts, and later in the federal Occupational Safety and Health Act). In the late twentieth century one must define the legal terms of corporate structure and governance by reference both to corporation law as such and to an increasingly influential body of regulatory law external to corporate organization. Some of this law bears immediately on the constitution of the market; some of it bears mainly on care for the social context of market activity.[124]

The corporation was not indispensable to the growth of market activity. Through much of the nineteenth century the typical form for sizeable business organizations was the partnership. Much of what businessmen did to arrange their affairs by using the corporate form they had earlier shown they could do through the ordinary law of contract or by adaptations of the trust device.[125] Yet, incorporation fast became the norm from the last quarter of the nineteenth century. At first, many business corporations simply succeeded what had been partnerships. But new technologies, the promise of economies of scale, the challenge of broader markets from expanding population within the protection of the federal system, and the ambitions of promoters invited entrepreneurs into larger enterprises than the country had ever before seen. As Andrew Carnegie demonstrated, it was possible to conduct a big business without incorporating it. But few followed Carnegie's example. From its origins the typical large enterprise was a corporation.[126]

The corporate form has served to increase market activity by assisting entrepreneurs to muster scattered capital and to control its use when it has been assembled. The two functions have proved to be at first complementary and later in some tension with each other. Before the rise of big business corporations law tended to emphasize recruiting capital by building into corporate structure various protections for investors and creditors, as by limits on corporate life and purposes and by stipulations to assure creation and maintenance of a core capital fund. Then development of the investment banking business reached out to much broader bodies of passive investors. Elaboration of more sophisticated contract and data-collection arrangements to protect lenders reduced pressure to focus corporation law on creditor interests.[127] The corporation income tax became a material factor in business calculations in the twentieth century. In this setting the favors which tax law afforded for management to meet much of its capital needs from retained earnings was a new element which tended to reduce attention to investor interests.[128] The counterpart of these currents of affairs was greater emphasis in incorporation statutes on assuring more freedom of decision to corporate management. Building on New Jersey and Delaware innovations of late nineteenth century, by the 1930s the norm of general incorporation laws was to structure the internal governance of the corporation to enable management, or management plus influential minority shareholders, to exercise broad discretion in fixing the financial, production, marketing, and growth policies of the enterprise.[129] This shift in policy has gone far enough to provoke response outside corporation law proper. Laws external to the corporation regulate a broadening range of its market activities as these affect investors, bond holders, labor, suppliers and franchised dealers, and consumers.[130]

Use of the corporate device for twentieth-century big business enterprise has both increased and restricted extension of market bargaining. Like the law of agency, of secured business and consumer debt, of dealer franchising, and of collective bargaining, incorporation has facilitated a larger firm than entrepreneurs had conceived before the 1880s. Thus, incorporation has assisted rapid growth in the volume, diversity, and geographical reach of private market operations, climaxing in the activities of multinational business corporations of the late twentieth century. Yet, in contrast, by contributing to increases in the size of business organizations incorporation has helped remove many resource allocations decisions from arenas of bargained transactions in the market, placing them instead within the internal hierarchy of the firm. Here, superiors planned and ordered allocations, and subordinates helped to plan and execute the firm's programs. To this extent private bureaucracy has supplanted private markets.[131] We should not draw this contrast in unrealistically sharp lines. In private as in public bureaucracies subordinates may materially affect and limit the effective direction of their superiors. Typically, within the ranks of a large firm there is give-and-take somewhat analogous to the give-and-take of markets. Granted this element, nonetheless the growth of big enterprises with the aid of incorporation has substantially reduced the volume and importance of resource allocations accomplished wholly by market bargaining, and increased allocations made through the discipline of private organizations.

CHAPTER 2

The Market in Social Context

Swelling currents of private business made the market a key institution in the United States. But it never stood alone, nor did it ever alone fix the course of public policy. Prevailing opinion put high priority on using law to foster the flow of private transactions. But support of particular transactions was not the law's only concern. Lawmakers acted also to promote the vitality of the market as a general institution of social order and to adjust its roles to those of other institutions. The market derived its vigor, however, from hard-driving energies of individual and group will and ambition. The source of its dynamic inevitably created tensions with values other than those readily defined through private bargaining for profit. Response—and failures of response—to these tensions made up a substantial part of the legal history of the market, especially from the last quarter of the nineteenth century.

COMMONWEALTH AND INDIVIDUAL VALUES

People in the United States are not much given to philosophizing about their values. But in practice, if to a less extent in expression, politically effective sectors of the society have shown that they hold some broadly shared ideas and feelings about themselves as a social whole, held together and working through accommodation among a range of ends and means supported by politically prevailing option.

Legal history reflects this sense of society—of the reality of values resident in some ideas of "commonwealth." In constituent acts those who prevailed demonstrated that what they wanted from life required substantial investment of calculated effort to deal with their social experience as a whole. Thus, they sought to bring into workable order a range of shared concerns embracing political, religious, social, and economic dimensions of living in common. This pattern appears in the Mayflower Compact, the Declaration of Independence, the several state constitutions, and the national Constitution. Social and individual values mingled in the determination that "[w]e, the people of the United States" would act "in order to form a more perfect union, establish justice, insure domestic tranquillity, provide for the common defence, promote the general welfare and secure the blessings of liberty to ourselves and our posterity."[1]

Landmark statutes recurrently responded to felt needs of the social fabric. That pattern holds together such otherwise disparate measures as Jefferson's Virginia statute on religious toleration (1786), the Northwest Ordinance (1787), the Massachusetts law of 1852 for compulsory attendance at public schools, the Homestead Act (1862), the Sherman Act (1890), the Federal Reserve Act (1913), and the Employment Act of 1946.[2]

The courts have given particularly focused attention to law's proper concern with commonwealth values in upholding the constitutionality of state legislation enacted under the "police power." This formula has more often declared a result than explained it. At its best, however, the canon points to the legitimacy of using law to promote the good order of relations on behalf of a humane life in society. Such was the import of a classic statement of Chief Justice Shaw for the Massachusetts Supreme Judicial Court in 1851: "The police power [is] . . . the power vested in the legislature by the Constitution, to make, ordain, and establish all manner of wholesome and reasonable laws, statutes, and ordinances, whether with penalties or without, not repugnant to the Constitution, as they shall judge to be for the good and welfare of the Commonwealth and of [its] subjects." Placing the market within its social context, Shaw observed that this legislative authority entered into and qualified all rights of property and contract, because "it is a settled principle, growing out of the nature of well-ordered civil society" that this relation should obtain. Thus, "[r]ights of property, like all other social and conventional rights, are subject to such reasonable limitations in their enjoyment, as shall prevent them from being injurious, and to such reasonable restraints and regulations established by law, as the legislature, under the governing and controlling power vested in them by the Constitution, may think necessary and expedient."[3] This emphasis on regard for the social context of the private market found another expression through Justice Holmes: "All rights tend to declare themselves absolute to their logical extreme. Yet all in fact are limited by the neighborhood of principles of policy which are other than those on which the particular right is founded, and which become strong enough to hold their own when a certain point is reached. The limits set to property by other public interests present themselves as a branch of what is called the police power of the State."[4]

Commonwealth goods involve matters of a generalized, collective charcter. But in this culture the context of values within which the market must fit has included also a high premium put on the quality and security of individual life. Though there have been inescapable tensions between the claims of society and those of the individual, experience has taught that they are not all beyond resolution. The individual and the society are interdependent, in large measure mutually sustaining, not necessarily antagonistic. Some nineteenth-century thinking might suggest that the individual gained by whatever public policy subtracted from social claims, and that society added to its strength whenever policy narrowed the scope available to individual will. However, a more realistic assessment of our experience of peace or turmoil in different social situations suggests that a good order of relations has been positive for both elements; the cul-

ture enriches individual life, but the individual is also the carrier
of shared values and is creative in developing them.[5]

Constitutional structure showed that our tradition prized individuality even as it provided for social peace. Bill of Rights protections against abuse of the state's penal processes—provision
of trial by jury and guarantees against compelled self-incrimina-
tion or unreasonable searches and seizures, for example—embodied the judgment that society should take risks with social
order out of regard for the worth of the individual. To this extent market claims that tradeable titles and assets be secure
against the thief must yield to protections for the accused individual. The judge-made and statute law of crimes, torts, and
contracts has involved analogous balancing of interests. Overall,
these bodies of law have bulwarked market dealing. But they
have also enforced respect for individuality. The burden of persuasion has fallen on one who seeks to avoid enforcement of a
private trading agreement, to show grounds for pronouncing it
against public policy; the law presumes private initiatives of will
to be free of wrongful intent, until the contrary be shown. So the
burden of persuasion has rested on one who seeks civil redress
for intentional or unintentional harm caused by another, to
show that the defendant's conduct should be deemed antisocial.
The courts will not convict of theft one not shown to have acted
with intent wrongfully to deprive the owner of his goods.[6] The
market's claims must at some point accommodate to the individual's claims for security against abuse of legal process. Concern for individual worth thus has been woven into concern for
commonwealth values.

MARKET CHARACTERISTICS AT ODDS WITH
COMMONWEALTH AND INDIVIDUAL VALUES

Some operating characteristics of the private market have
proved inconsistent with accepting it as a self-sufficient agency

of social control. Left wholly to its own devices the market is capable not only of generating problems of efficiency for its immediate goals but also of creating issues of social welfare not measurable by a market calculus. Experience of these limitations has shown the need of some intervention from outside the market to relate it to a broader context of social organization and individual claims. In the second half of the twentieth century a catalog of operational limitations of the market has become a familiar element in economic theory.[7] The legal record provides no startling amendment of the economists' analysis. But the legal record does add its own confirmation of the existence and gravity of market limitations, since their felt presence has overcome the normal inertias of government, producing wide response in statute, administrative, and judge-made law.

Developments in the law have reflected perception of four limitations on the market's capacity to mesh well with the general social context. These limitations involve (1) the restricted range of interests immediately moving market action, (2) the constrictions of a money calculus, (3) the market's bias toward continuing but limited incremental change, and (4) the market's acceptance or promotion of inequalities in distribution of economic, social, and political power.

Focus of Interests

The market gets its driving energy from the focused wills of those who bargain out transactions for their own profit. This dynamic means that, left to pursue its own course, the market will take account only of a narrow range of interests potentially affected by the bargainers' transactions. This aspect of affairs did not make itself felt much so long as population was thin relative to unopened land, cities were few and small-town living was relatively simple, and communications, production, and distribution not yet developed on a great scale. Demands on law grew as people perceived that denser and more interlocked processes of living caused particular transactions to affect the well-being of many outside the circle of bargainers. In close urban settings, infected milk or polluted water was not simply cause of private complaint; through epidemics such defective goods or contaminated resources could imperil the whole community. Though for a long time tardy and poorly implemented, the law of public health and sanitation nonetheless expanded from the mid-nineteenth century to impose substantial conditions on the marketing of foodstuffs in the interests not only of immediate consumers but also of their neighbors.[8] Through most of the nineteenth century manufacturers were in practice free to build factories at streamside to use rivers as handy, apparently costless sewers to carry off industrial wastes. The price the maker charged his customers was the cheaper because it included no allowance for losses suffered by others who depended on the streams for drinking water or fish or healthful recreation. The closer terms of twentieth-century living have stirred more active concern for these detriments that fall outside the typical contract calculations of sellers and buyers of the factory's output. In the twentieth century, statutes and administrative rules under statutory delegation have begun to enforce redefinition of costs of production to cover expenditures necessary to protect the purity of water.[9] Analogous currents of policy, from crude legislative beginnings in the late nineteenth century into more sophisticated administrative regulations a hundred years later, began to require that industry include in its costs of production the expenditures needed to reduce air pollution from industrial wastes, to guard the safety and health of the work force, to reduce dangers involved in transporting hazardous materials, and—most belated of all such measures—to provide safe conditions of storage of dangerous chemical residues resulting from production operations.[10] Such legal regulation has increased in the face of continuing controversy. The fact attests that politically effective opinion has found the market too narrowly oriented to be accepted as legitimate on its own terms in a tightly interlocked community.[11] The course of policy bore out the summary of Justice Holmes: "In modern societies every part is related so organically to every other that what affects any portion must be felt more or less by all the rest. Therefore, unless everything is to be forbidden and legislation is to come to a stop, it is not enough to show that in the working of a statute there is some tendency logically discernible to interfere with commerce or existing contracts. Practical lines have to be drawn and distinctions of degree must be made."[12]

A Monetized Calculus

Large-scale, pervasive market activity cannot develop by barter; it must work through money, including credit measured in money units. For all its imperfections and through all its phases the country's money system has proved a potent instrument for extending the range and reach of markets. But even more than by its effects in promoting transactions, the use of money has had profound influence in fixing the terms in which people define and measure their options in allocating resources. Accustomed to everyday use of this instrument in making decisions, lawmakers have tended to limit the factors they weigh to those which translate readily into money-measured costs and yields determined within the frame of private bargaining for money-measured profit. By subtle bias of habit even more than by explicit formula, that approach tends to exclude from the rationale of choice those elements which private bargaining cannot easily define and measure in money units. The money calculus especially has inclined decisionmakers to exclude from calculation objective factors of the physical, biological, and social environment appraised for their in-fact, cause-and-effect impacts on life; in this sense a money calculus has encouraged individuals to ignore or subordinate real factors for which money measurement was at best only a symbol.[13]

The shaping influence of a money calculus was reflected in the nineteenth century in the sharp disjunction between elaborate development of redress for individual complainants in property, contract, and tort law, and the scant doctrine available to protect real but diffuse economic or social interests. Courts were comfortable in assessing money damages for commission of trespass or private nuisance to the detriment of a particular landowner, or in enjoining a third party's wrongful interference with a private contract relation, or in giving judgment for money damages for fraud or deceit practiced by one private bargainer upon another. In such situations the law and the parties' behavior produced closely defined and limited relationships involving elements familiar in private bargains and thus amenable to money measurement. But where both the socially productive interests at stake and the detriments were broadly shared, without sharp distinction of particular impacts on particular persons, money reckonings were difficult if not impossible. Judges and legislators often either did not see such situations as involving any legally relevant rights or duties of anyone, or they lacked the skill or motive to contrive new definitions of interests and new procedures to implement new definitions.[14] Symbolic was the narrow definition of security for the public interest regarding Wisconsin's disposal of its publicly owned timberlands. When the state sold such land in fee simple on credit, it imposed on the buyer restrictions on timber cutting until he paid the purchase price. But Wisconsin imposed no further regulations on the manner and scale of lumbering on land once the land was fully in private ownership. That there might be a commonwealth interest in preserving the forest as a self-sustaining productive resource of the general economy was an idea outside nineteenth-century policy concepts, bounded as these tended to be by preoccupation with servicing particularized, money-measured transactions.[15]

By contrast, two developments in twentieth-century law affecting the market highlight how far the monetized calculus of interests limited nineteenth-century public policy. No change bulked larger in the legal order after 1900 than the rise of the administrative process, as statutes delegated broad rule-making and adjudicatory powers to agencies regulating the marketing of transport, electric power, communications, food and drugs, and a wide range of other goods and services, as well as regulating conditions of labor, and ultimately the protection of the physical and biological environment. Some of this growth could be explained as providing more effective remedies for particular grievances of market bargainers who lacked practical power to invoke conventional contract, property, or tort doctrine for their protection. But the range of this new style of legal intervention was too sweeping and the investment of public resources too large to be explained simply on this basis. Sustaining and broadening the growth of administrative process were new-felt concerns with commonwealth interests—in social peace, in integrity of the society's resource base, in preservation of the market itself as a functioning institution. This new chapter of legal history in effect repudiated the monetized calculus as sufficient of itself to define the aspects of market operations relevant to the social context.[16] More limited in impact, but likewise signalling dissatisfaction with older money measures of legally recognized claims, has been late-twentieth-century expansion of definitions of those deemed to have legal standing to seek decisions from courts on contested interests. Judges have now begun to entertain suits brought on behalf of large classes of individuals to safeguard commonwealth interests in conserving natural resources, protecting against air or water pollution, or maintaining the natural beauty of the countryside. True, the litigant must show that the challenged situation had some direct, objectively identifiable impact on him. But the Supreme Court has been prepared to give an expansive reading to this requirement; thus, it ruled that individuals who use such environmental resources as public parks have standing to sue to obtain a railroad rate structure calculated to encourage recycling of industrial raw materials and so to reduce litter.[17] To recognize standing in such petitioners for such claims reaches far beyond older requirements that a litigant show in himself a substantial, money-measured stake within the categories of rights defined by the conventional law of property, contract, or tort.[18]

The Weight of Incremental Change

Most of the time market dealing is a process of many continuing, relatively limited adjustments by particular operators to shifting circumstances of supply and demand. This is not a necessary or invariable condition. Particular operators may make striking innovations of great general impact, as when Henry Ford introduced a low-priced automobile through assembly-line production. Moreover, though market dealing alone may not regularly produce major change, legal protection gives scope for private initiative and for extending the quantity and geographical scale of bargaining. Within that protection the market is a potent agent for transmitting and amplifying influences that originate outside it. These transmitting and amplifying effects have been most powerfully felt in helping technological innovation to change social structure, political alignments, and cultural values. Nonetheless, the general tendency of market calculations has created a bias toward change that is continuing, though usually of a relatively undramatic, inconspicuous, incremental kind. Deliberate, large-scale, planned change spells more risk than most market operators care to assume.[19]

If market changes moved only within a narrow range and regularly returned to equilibrium about a familiar norm, public policy probably would have used law simply to facilitate and protect the routine of transactions. But in this shifting, ambitious culture, politically influential opinion has not been content with a steady state of the economy; through the corporation, the money supply, and federalism we have used law to extend markets, and hence inevitably to reshape the character of the market as an institution of social control and to alter other aspects of society affected by the changing market. However, different problems went with the mingling of two kinds of change—

change sought through deliberate, large-scale efforts to structure the market and its relation to the whole society, and change worked by accumulation of continuing, small increments of difference through great flows of particular transactions.

Deliberate, large-scale structuring attracted the concentrated attention of lawmakers and interest groups. Thus, not surprisingly, high controversy centered on Jackson's veto of a renewed charter for the second Bank of the United States, as it did later on Woodrow Wilson's jousting with bankers over terms on which Congress would create the Federal Reserve System. Massive social consequences can also follow from accumulation of change by small increments through what appear to be routine operations of the market. Because that kind of influence has moved through familiar currents of everyday experience, typically it has not gained public policy attention until the community has found itself substantially committed to a condition of affairs it had not perceived in the course of formation, had never deliberated, and had never chosen as a desired goal. Thus fifty years of mass production and mass marketing of automobiles and trucks, heavily subsidized by public spending on hard-surfaced roads, contributed to reduce the role and financial health of the country's railroads, to promote the sprawling growth of urban areas and socially divisive separation of central city and suburbs, to multiply costs of personal injury, to imperil health through air pollution, and to increase the society's dangerous dependence on oil as a source of energy. Such factors did not establish that social costs outweighed social gains to an extent that condemned mass marketing of autos and trucks. But from the standpoint of good social order, the point was one of process: market operations thus restructured the society and altered the quality of people's lives in major respects without ever presenting these changes to be identified, weighed, and chosen, rejected, or modified, in a forum broad enough to match the stakes.[20]

The hazards that can flow from unguided commitments effected through massed results of fragmented market dealing have found response in some twentieth-century shifts in uses of law. John Locke's principles emphasized individual will and stipulated that the individual should not have to obtain an official license before he engaged in economically productive activity. In contrast, twentieth-century policy has brought increased centralization of decisionmaking through official procedures—largely to match the rise of centralized private decisionmaking—and has made substantial use of licensing procedures to assure that society's experience will not be determined simply by the drift of market transactions. Expansion of the administrative process has been part of this new style of social control. Legislation has delegated economic regulatory powers to specialized agencies largely because lawmakers have felt the need to bring sustained, specialized official will to bear on marketing activity, which, however closely directed by the dealers to their immediate ends, is not shaped by them in terms of total social impact. Such developments have been particularly marked in legal regulation of more sophisticated modes of producing and selling foods and drugs, or of multiplied use of chemicals in industrial processes. Statute law has thus reflected judgments that the community could not safely allow the market alone to decide applications of new technologies. Too often these situations have involved knowledge so far outside common understanding and effects so diffuse or postponed (however serious in overall consequences) that individuals have lacked the motivation or competence to bargain out their own protections. Experience has shown that there has been considerable naivete in the high expectations held out for the accomplishments of administrative agencies. But this lesson does not negate the distrust of market processes which has lain behind the resort to the new style of legal regulation.[21]

In a simpler time norms of common law supported Locke's rejection of official licensing. Thus, the fee simple title originally conferred on the owner broad discretion to decide what use he would make of his land, and the law of contract presumed the legality of private agreements. Licensing carries dangers that special interests will use licensing laws to fend off competition that might benefit the public. Nonetheless, twentieth-century legislators have turned to licensing and inspection procedures on a large scale. In some part they have thus made undesirable concessions to special-interest lobbies. But this explanation cannot account for much of the reach of modern licensing procedures. In substantial measure these have been intended to forestall or control damaging results that might flow from unguided, incremental changes worked by market activity. Thus, twentieth-century policy has curtailed the freedom of the owner in fee simple, first by urban and later by rural zoning ordinances. In the late twentieth century the law has reversed Locke's no-license principle by requiring official clearances for marketing new medicines and for developing industrial uses of nuclear power, and is cautiously moving toward controls on basic research in genetic engineering. Thus, the most confident expansion of licensing has focused on social impacts of technological change. There, people have become most aware that sheer drift of market-borne currents can basically reshape or even imperil their lives. Yet policy here has continued in flux. In the 1980s movements to reduce public regulation and enlarge scope for market competition in transportation and communications have shown that Locke's no-license principle still carries persuasive force.[22]

The Market as an Instrument of Inequality in Power

Market allocations have implicitly accepted private decision-making within an existing structure of power. The market's function is to maximize current exercise of private will in transactions. This preoccupation encourages private interests and lawmakers alike to beg questions of the effects which unequal distribution of wealth and income have on people's relative opportunities to exercise private initiative of will.

In most respects dissatisfaction with market processes in their broad impacts on society have developed more sharply in the twentieth than in the nineteenth century. Concentration on the immediate interests of the bargainers, emphasis on interests measurable in money, acceptance or unawareness of incremental change worked through dispersed transactions—these features of market processes were not felt as sources of major strain in a relatively simple economy and in a culture which valued the means the market provided for expressing prized initiatives of individual will. It took the rapid growth of closer social interdependence and belated perception of postponed costs of market-borne change after 1900 to generate pronounced worry over products of these aspects of market operations. In contrast, however, substantial controversy marched with the course of affairs from 1790 on regarding market influences on unequal distribution of wealth and income and the political and social alignments which contributed to and were shaped by inequalities. As early as *Federalist* No. 10 Madison noted that "the most common and durable source of factions has been the various and unequal distribution of property." In this fact he saw continuing need that law intervene: "The regulation of these various and interfering interests forms the principal task of modern legislation and involves the spirit of party and faction in the necessary and ordinary operations of the government." He was quickly borne out, as controversy attended Hamilton's programs for refunding the public debt in ways which critics saw as favoring the wealthy to the prejudice of ordinary folk.[23]

Criticism might pursue two counts: one, that the market contributes materially to creating economic inequality; second, that where it does not create inequality it does not provide a reliable means for redressing inequality, but is more likely to entrench it. In fact the record is mixed—mixed enough so that realistic appraisal cannot simply label the market an instrument or a bulwark of oppression.

The Anglo-American tradition has valued the private market and the law's protection of its relative autonomy as contributors to civil liberty. This doctrine has taught that assets acquired in market dealing—the fee simple title to a commercial farm, the capital of a business—and livelihood gained from occupations that require no official license to serve private customers nerve and arm individuals to play roles in public affairs and if necessary to oppose mistakes or abuse of official power.[24] Healthy dispersion of power in public policymaking also derives largely from diverse private associations—ranging from political parties to business firms, trade associations, trade unions, farmers' organizations, and lobbies for general community interests in health, recreation, or resource conservation. Such associations have maintained themselves in part with money which donors have acquired directly or indirectly through market processes. Indeed, in the late twentieth century most individuals who support such public interest groups as Common Cause or the Sierra Club or the NAACP have involved themselves mainly by sending their checks to the organizations.[25] The Supreme Court has in effect recognized this civil liberties contribution of the market in the breadth of First Amendment protection it has cast about private political contributions and private lobbying activity.[26] In a more limited sphere, market competition, especially as reinforced by technological change, has remained vigorous enough to effect sometimes dramatic shifts or even disappearances among the ranks of big business. Such alterations most immediately affect only rank ordering within the sphere of corporate enterprise. Yet, given the importance of large corporations in the twentieth-century United States, such discipline as market competition has created tempered inequalities of power.

Nonetheless, of course, aggressive private operators have used market gains to build preeminent practical power for themselves in markets and in public arenas. From such vantage points they have pursued profit according to their own criteria of propriety.

In its administrative flexibility and reach the market has offered great leverage for accumulating and concentrating wealth or control of wealth. Moreover, the focus of the private market is on allocating resources to produce and distribute goods and services for sale, not on determining suitable standards for distributing ultimate life satisfactions. Thus, pursuing its ordinary working goals, insofar as it has not fostered growth of inequality of wealth or incomes, market activity has tended to support enjoyment of superior economic power wherever superior power already existed.[27]

In two principal forms public policy has reflected concern with these aspects of the private market. One has been resort to regulatory law to build countervailing centers of bargaining power through private associations. This has been one goal of legal protection of collective bargaining in labor relations. On the other hand, lawmakers have undertaken to create countervailing centers of bargaining power through specialized official action, as in the mingling of command and negotiation that characterizes the Antitrust Division of the Department of Justice or the Federal Trade Commission. Another official approach has been through government's taxing and spending authority to effect transfers of purchasing power by law, notably in public welfare programs or through public contracts. Growth in government's regulatory and fiscal roles has measured the extent to which politically effective opinion has refused to accept market processes as unquestioned arbiters of the general structure of power.[28]

PUBLIC POLICY TO CURB SELF-DESTRUCTIVE TENDENCIES IN THE MARKET

Law has played two quite different parts in support of the market. In the ordinary law of property, contract, and tort, and in its provision of incorporation, a federal structure, and a standardized money supply, the legal system has helped sustain and expand a regular on-going course of transactions for private profit. In this facilitative role law has been effective because and insofar as it worked within customs, habits, ethical norms, and shared expectations established not by legal fiat but by people's continuing, practical experience in organizing production and distribution through bargaining. These uses of law have accepted the market as a sustained pattern of action already given by growth of the culture; in this aspect law has simply undertaken to assist execution of particular operations within the given institution.

Yet, the market exists within a social context that includes needs and demands of other institutions and other goals than those immediately served by particular bargains for private profit. Experience has taught that some operating characteristics of the private market put its results at serious odds with nonmarket elements of the social context. These tensions have generated demands for legal intervention in the private market for other than facilitative ends.

A prime lesson we have had to learn in this connection was that, though law does not create the market, law may be needed to keep the market itself in being. This is a sobering caution. At least since the seventeenth century Anglo-American political tradition has relied on the private market not only as an instrument to allocate limited economic resources in producing and distributing goods and services, but also to help keep social peace by contributing to a humane balance of power between government and private interests and by promoting constructive outlets for creative energy of individual will.[29] As an element of social order the market is part of the social context, and experience has shown that the market itself can be imperilled because routines of market dealing may not correct self-destructive tendencies developed in the course of business. Thus, not to facilitate ordinary market dealing, but rather to help keep the market in being, public policy became concerned with problems of (1) mutuality in bargaining, (2) concentration of private control of assets, and (3) costs attending major shifts in the business cycle.

Mutuality

A vital market requires that dealers enjoy reasonable freedom of choice relative to each other. If one set of actors habitually perform according to the will of another set, the situation spells hierarchy and not bargain. A continuing market presupposes that most participants find an acceptable measure of net satisfaction in their transactions. Powered as it is by the self-interest of transacting parties, the market is imperilled when some dealers can regularly exploit gross inequalities of bargaining position.

The oldest line of policy concerned with extreme departures from mutuality in market dealing was fixed by judge-made law and—as might be expected from doctrine developed in litigation—was fashioned only to the circumstances of particular transactions. At common law courts normally refused to examine the substantive adequacy of what a party bargained for in an exchange; if the stated consideration or an exchange met judge-made formal tests indicating that the parties intended a firm transaction, that ended the matter. Occasionally common law courts would find that gross inadequacy of consideration was persuasive evidence of fraud or of breach of an implied warranty of quality, and thus provided a defense against enforcing a contract. But such occasions were marginal to the common law's general favor for enforcing agreements as written.[30] On the other hand, in doctrine stretching back into the eighteenth century, courts of Equity asserted capacity to relieve a party from what the court deemed an unconscionably harsh contract. The Uniform Commercial Code (2-302) carries a counterpart authorization into twentieth-century legislation. But since the legislation simply declares a broad standard of fairness, in practice its realization has remained a matter of judge-made law, specific to the circumstances of particular cases. Moreover, this equitable defense is rarely effective.[31]

Great expansion of market transactions has depended in fact and in law on reliable standardization of terms of dealing. The ways in which policymakers have used law to facilitate market growth has shown that their principal bias has been to assure legal support of contracts, rather than call it into question. Thus it is not surprising that common law and Equity doctrine policing against unduly one-sided contracts have had only marginal impact. Even so, the fact that in the general climate of policy some doctrine against unconscionable transactions existed at all attested that lawmakers sensed self-destructive possibilities in the market.

The growth of a special body of statutory public utility law marked much broader legal intervention to redress inequalities of bargaining position in private markets. The determining factor here has been the insecurity of scattered interests subject to exactions of private powerholders standing at key points of business traffic. In *Munn* v. *Illinois* (1876) the Supreme Court held that the state legislature had reasonable basis, consistent with the due process clause of the Fourteenth Amendment, for finding that law would serve the public interest by regulating maximum charges for storage of grain in warehouses in Chicago and other major collecting points. For the Court Chief Justice Waite identified the critical element as the factual structure of the parties' relationships: "[A]ll the elevating facilities through which these vast productions 'of seven or eight great States of the West' must pass on the way 'to four or five of the States on the seashore' may be a 'virtual' monopoly. . . . [The regulated grain elevators] stand, to use again the language of their counsel, in the very 'gateway of commerce', and take toll from all who pass."[32] The threat to the integrity of the market was the presence of centralized private control of facilities intermediate in the chain of production and distribution, on which many more dispersed market activities depended.

Until the late twentieth century public utility law developed toward increasing legal involvement with regulated industries. Massachusetts' pioneer railroad regulation under Charles Francis Adams (1869) relied largely on the sanction of publicity. The first direct regulation of railroad rates under the Granger laws of midwestern states fixed charges in the statute books. Experience soon taught that this approach was impacticable. By the turn of the century the standard type of regulation was by statutory delegation to specialized administrative bodies which created highly detailed, technical bodies of regulations and schedules. Such remained the norm until the 1980s saw reassessment of the range of regulation in transport and communications, spurred by concern to encourage more industry initiative in competition. It seems a reasonable prophecy, however, that regulation will remain a major factor on behalf of public interests in safety and in nondiscriminatory provision of key services. The course of public utility law has reflected shifting appraisals of defects and qualities of the range, variety, and flexibility of bargaining possible through private market processes. The market's character has called for generalizing regulatory policy and yet adapting it in detail to complex situations, while respecting the capacities of market competition for promoting innovation and disciplining performance.[33]

Such redress as Equity or common law afforded against unconscionable deals judged the unique character of particular transactions. In effect statutory public utility law began with a like focus on the individual case, though it did not do so openly. Early-nineteenth-century franchises for such key-point facilities as navigation improvements authorized proprietors to charge tolls, but might stipulate only that tolls be reasonable. In effect such a formula remitted an aggrieved customer to a lawsuit, the outcome of which would depend on the particular record built by that suitor. This approach could build only slowly toward correcting inequalities of bargaining power common to classes of those dependent on the public utility. The method was too expensive and fragmented to work. The mainline of growth in public utility law soon took more of a legislative than an adjudicative direction. Regulations intended to promote reasonable and nondiscriminatory rates and services undertook to structure dealings by classifications of like situations, rather than by responding to individualized complaints.[34]

This turn toward emphasizing broad structures of market relationships carried implications for a wider range of issues than those encountered in the conventional categories of public utilities. Like questions of the legitimacy of the market could rise wherever centralized private control of large enterprises confronted diffuse interests on the other side of the table. Such broader problems developed in management-labor relations in big firms, and in dealings between big firms and large bodies of unorganized small businesses, small investors, and ultimate consumers. The response in public policy, which reached beyond the familiar catalog of public utilities, was to interpose new forms of collective power between concentrated centers of entrepreneurial and managerial decisionmaking and dispersed bodies of small bargainers.[35] On behalf of small business, small investors, and ordinary consumers, legislatures placed new intermediate power in official agencies, to which they delegated authority to regulate for safety and quality and against fraud in marketing foods, drugs, technical services, franchises and corporate securities.[36] On behalf of wage earners, policy took both direct and indirect approaches. Directly, legislation provided for regulation to protect the health and safety of workers and to fix standards for hours and wages. Indirectly, law offered legal protection of collective bargaining to help trade unions furnish the intermediate structure of power between management and labor.[37] As in so many other respects, this was a movement of public policy which marked sharp differences between the years before and after the 1880s.

In the twentieth century differences between large and small employers have created another dimension of problems. Some of the worst offenders against decent working conditions have been small employers. They are not likely to be more grasping or conscienceless than other people. But chronic shortage of investment and working capital and the short tether on which their creditors keep them have made them more desperately vulnerable to competition. Trade union organization has had some success in offsetting these pressures in the garment industry.[38] But union organization is too costly to provide answers across the board for small business management-labor relations. Despite the administrative burdens entailed, direct legal regulation has proved the only practical response in most such situations. Even there, experience dictates exemptions below some size of firm.[39] The cost of compliance—in recordkeeping, inspections, response to required changes in equipment or operating methods —can bear relatively more heavily on the budgets of small firms. The fact does not warrant wholesale exemptions of small business from meeting some standards of fair dealing in the labor market. But as the weight of labor regulation increased in the later twentieth century, the reality of differential impacts of regulation on different-sized firms has contributed to the pressure from business for more closely calculating costs relative to benefits of regulatory effort.[40]

Business Concentration

According to the classical explanation vigorous competition is the dynamic which legitimizes the private market as an institution of social control. Insofar as competition has performed this function, it has made the market a risky arena in which to commit assets. Understandably, some business firms may prefer to escape or at least reduce hazards by achieving monopoly power, or by intimidating competition by force or fraud, or by striking treaties of accommodation with each other. Ever the realist, Adam Smith had recognized that the market contained such self-destructive tendencies.[41] Up to the late nineteenth century, however, law in the United States showed little response to this threat. The principal exception was manifest in jealousy of special privilege gained by businessmen through statutory franchises, such as Andrew Jackson displayed in vetoing renewal of the charter of the second Bank of the United States.[42] So far as law condemned some private dealings as contracts in restraint of trade, generally it simply refused to enforce them—a quite passive response to dynamic drives.[43] But from about the 1880s the country experienced headlong growth of firms involving unprecedented scales of capital investment, organization, and marketing reach.[44] Compared with the scant development of doctrine protective of competition over the preceding century, the end of the nineteenth century saw a dramatic response to the declaration of new responsibilities of law. Through an ensuing critical generation of rapid economic change, however, there was little effective effort to fulfill the new role. Meanwhile, the commerce clause protected business in its reach into broad domestic markets; liberalized corporation laws made the corporate device available for massing capital on terms substantially set by entrepreneurs; and through decades important for the growth of enterprise, low levels of taxation facilitated plowback of earnings for the further concentration of assets.

Despite ineffective enforcement the Sherman Act (1890) symbolized new-felt concern for the social functions of the market. It was no longer enough that law should facilitate market transactions; the Sherman Act recognized that government must take positive responsibility to keep private competition alive. Further, reflecting the unprecedented scale of operations of the new breed of enterprises, the act recognized that only the national government could muster the resources to deal with such private concentrations of economic, social, and political influence. In 1895, when it ruled that the act did not (and, the indication was, might not constitutionally) apply to a combination of industrial enterprises, the Supreme Court appeared to confine the Sherman

Act to the area of interstate transportation.[45] But Presidents Theodore Roosevelt and William Howard Taft brought fresh executive initiatives into play, presenting judges with opportunities which they seized, to reconsider and interpret the act in terms to make it apply wherever private combinations materially affected markets of interstate reach.[46] By the 1920s the Court had confirmed that the Sherman Act warranted national action to preserve competitive vitality in all types of major markets.[47] By 1933, in the *Appalachian Coals* opinion, the Supreme Court was ready to accept the act as a policy pronouncement of scope comparable to constitutional guarantees.[48] The characterization was an apt reminder that since the late seventeenth century Anglo-American policy had not valued the private market simply as an instrument of efficient resource allocation. That tradition depended on the market also as a component of a desired balance of power between private and public centers affecting general political and social as well as economic structure. Antitrust law recast the tradition in terms of a vastly altered society.

For over forty years, to enforce the Sherman Act and its supplements, the United States made no investment even moderately commensurate with the challenge. A turning point came between 1938 and 1941, when Assistant Attorney General Thurman Arnold built the first substantial Antitrust Division in the Department of Justice. World War II shelved the expanded effort. But the Arnold legacy remained and was consolidated after 1950. By the 1980s federal antitrust enforcement was a substantial, continuing, professional enterprise of the Department of Justice and a reinvigorated Federal Trade Commission.[49]

This stronger antitrust effort worked within the constraints of an earlier legacy, however. From the 1890s into the 1930s the economy developed a pattern of a handful of large firms dominating trade in particular markets. A few successful lawsuits to break up particular mergers or restrictive agreements only marginally affected emergence of the new styles of market structures and processes. True, antitrust accomplishments in the span from 1890 to 1938 were not negligible. The federal effort was enough to define and legitimate bans and penalties on some predatory types of competition, such as geographic price discrimination, or use of fighting brands or espionage.[50] Decisions established that overt price-fixing agreements among competitors were in themselves violations of the Sherman Act, whether or not the price-fixers showed reasonable self restraint.[51] By the 1930s, however, it was clear that antitrust policy would coexist with an economy in which firms of great size were major factors and in which, in particular markets, a handful of firms would account for 40 percent or more of the goods and services dealt in.

Within the expanded antitrust enforcement that followed World War II, the basic structure of the economy did not change. But within that framework what went on was subject to closer government scrutiny and more risk of government intervention than had existed before 1938. Economists debated how much market power large firms possessed, and how far competition—albeit in forms other than through price—continued to impose its discipline.[52] Old style price-fixing agreements did not disappear: antitrust enforcers prosecuted through to consent decrees, or less frequently to judgments in civil or criminal contests, a continuing flow of actions against such overt efforts to subvert competition.[53] More subtle were developments in the law concerning behavior of principal actors in markets where four, six, or eight operators loomed large. One view of antitrust enforcement was that, without overt collusion, so few large operators, either with anticompetitive intent or under the pressure of individual interest, would tend to make pricing or other marketing decisions within limits set by the reactions they anticipated from the other firms. In the late twentieth century, antitrust enforcement was vigorous enough to put such market dealers at risk of legal sanctions if their behavior fell into patterns circumstantially persuasive of collusion, though the practical difficulties of proving a prosecution case left considerable leeway

for big firms quietly to coordinate their production and marketing programs.[54] It was hard to pass confident judgment on how
much distinct impact antitrust law had on the character of the
principal types of markets. Aside from specially regulated public
utilities, true monopoly was rare, and it seemed likely that the
threat of antitrust prosecution had materially curbed monopolis-
tic ambitions.[55] Otherwise, however, it seemed likely that technological innovation—including advances in science-based technology—operating within continuing favor for freedom of contract did as much as antitrust law after 1950 to keep competition
alive. We are usually closer to reality if we adopt a modest
estimate of the effects of law relative to other influences.[56]
Nonetheless, if antitrust law shared honors with science and
technology in preserving competition, the continuity of policy
since Thurman Arnold has indicated that federal antitrust enforcement was as permanent an element of twentieth-century
legal order as any other factor. Politically influential opinion
was not disposed to trust the market to maintain its competitive
discipline simply out of its own resources.

Some critics have charged that antitrust enforcement has been
harsher on small than on big business. In this view strict, no-
excuse-allowed condemnation of agreements among competing
firms fixing prices or apportioning sales territories might deny
small firms their only means of holding their position in market.
When an enterprise grew by merger, it was subject only to a
more flexible rule of reason in judging its legality. Where a few
big firms dominated a market, their size and limited number allowed them in practice to limit pricing or other forms of competition by less open collusion, which made successful prosecution more difficult.[57] Evidence does not permit assured judgments on these claims. But on the whole the criticisms do not
carry ready persuasion. The central objective of protecting competition warranted strictly condemning overt price-fixing arrangements, not only to punish but also to prevent growth of
concentrated private power. Up to the 1980s, antitrust policing

of mergers has not shown leniency toward bigness. On the record, most government actions against mergers have dealt with firms already large, seeking to increase their market shares.[58] Public policy bias favoring big business has shown itself less in antitrust law than in tax and patent law and in government contracting.[59]

Deflation and Inflation

Until the last quarter of the nineteenth century there was no substantial, sustained demand that government assume positive responsibilities to moderate, let alone manage, large changes in prices and in the overall volume and pace of market activity. The Federal Constitution effectively barred states from manipulating the supply of coin and currency. Before 1861 distrust of national legislative power assured that Congress would make no direct efforts to manage the money supply. Credit was the area left open for policy maneuver. The Supreme Court ruled that the Constitution's ban on state bills of credit did not bar the states from unlimited chartering of commercial banks authorized to issue circulating notes as well as to lend to businessmen. Subject to no centralized surveillance, several hundred state-chartered banks along with other private lenders expanded or restricted credit over widely and erratically varying ranges. When sharp downswings in the general course of business and business credit brought deflationary pressure on debtors, state legislatures from time to time passed temporary debtor relief laws, subject to curbs imposed by the Supreme Court under the contract clause of the national Constitution. This period showed no material state action concerned with inflation.[60]

The national government provided the one important exception to the tendency of public policy to let the general course of business run its own course under market discipline. Congress chartered the First (1791) and Second (1861) Banks of the United States as national monopoly banks empowered not only to serve the government as fiscal agents but also to issue circulating notes and to extend private credit. The Supreme Court ruled that Congress had constitutional authority to charter a national bank. For most of their lives the two national banks played no large managing role in the economy. But from 1824 to 1832 under Nicholas Biddle the Second Bank built a remarkable record in policing not only its own currency but also the notes of state-chartered banks, and managing the general supply of credit to adjust it to the overall movement of business, and especially to keep it in working alignment with changing geographical and seasonal demands. Brought down by the competitive jealousy of state-chartered banks and by Andrew Jackson's distrust of the extent of power so concentrated in a private corporation, the Second Bank did not obtain a renewal of its charter, and this experiment in central economic management thus expired.[61]

To help finance the North's war effort in 1863 and 1864 Congress enacted general acts for incorporating commercial banks under national charters. In 1866 through a prohibitive tax Congress drove out the circulating notes of state-chartered banks. This step was of no lasting detriment to the state banks, whose earnings now came from their lending activity, creating deposit-check money. The national bank acts created no authority or procedures for central supervision of the overall supply of money and credit; the principal regulatory activity under that legislation focused only on the solvency of individual banks.[62] Thus from 1832 until 1913 public policy—or, more accurately, the defaults of public policy—left to the governance of the private market overall shifts in the supply of money and credit and in the general course of business.[63] Save for the short-lived regime of Nicholas Biddle, the record suggests that little else could have been expected. Economic theory was rudimentary. Government was ill-equipped to devise macroeconomic programs. Policymakers had scant knowledge or theory for managing the money supply. Until near the end of the nineteenth century cash or cash equivalents were scarce enough so that taxation could not provide government much fiscal leverage on the economy. Neither the national government nor the state governments possessed a fund of administrative skill on which they could draw to carry out ambitious programs, had they had any. The limitations of policy direction were highlighted by the energy expended to no constructive effect in the political battles waged in the last quarter of the nineteenth century over retirement of the national government's Civil War fiat currency (the greenbacks), and the demand for free coinage of silver as against return to the gold standard. The closest the politics of the time could come to a more constructive program was the abortive drive of the Populists to obtain a legal frame for providing low-cost credit to farmers and small business.[64]

By the late nineteenth century the growth in scale and reach of market dealing made people increasingly vulnerable to major shifts in the course of the market, and more sharply aware of their vulnerability. Farmers, small businessmen, and workers suffered costly deprivations of their resources and their security, to an extent that made serious inroads on popular acceptance of the legitimacy of the private market and the legal system which supported it. The breadth of response to Henry George's *Progress and Poverty* (1879), to the Populist drive of the 1880s, and to the Bryan campaign of 1893, and the alarmed reactions of middle-class and upper-middle-class opinion to these movements, signalled that events were preparing a base of opinion to support more positive government intervention to preserve the market from the most damaging impacts of large swings in the general course of business.[65]

The creation of the Federal Reserve System in 1913 at last reversed Andrew Jackson's decision of 1832 and gave the country a central bank with the potential to regulate the supply of money and credit. Held back by want of effective economic theory, administrative experience, and will to take independent and decisive action, the system did not begin fully to realize its potential

until the 1950s. Then, by trial and error the Federal Reserve
Board finally undertook to develop its most flexible process for
managing the money supply, by purchases and sales of government securities.[66]

Under the hammer blows of the 1930s' depression, government set further precedents for intervening to keep the private
market in being. By spending on public works, by establishing
temporary public employment programs, and by creating systems
of unemployment insurance and social security, governments
drew on their taxing and spending powers in ways without par-
allel to restore and maintain private purchasing power. The national government took the country off the gold standard, to allow
more flexible control of the money supply. Congress provided
public loans to distressed banks and business firms, to farmers,
and to beleaguered homeowners. On a more limited scale, state
legislatures also acted against down-spiralling markets, through
price regulation, mortgage moratoria, and public relief and employment programs. The fiscal measures of the thirties proved
too hesitant to move the country out of its depressed condition;
action on a sufficient scale to do that derived not from domestic
policy but from rearmament to meet the threat posed by Hitler
and then from massive expenditures to fight World War II.
Nonetheless, the domestic actions of the 1930s created a new
frame of reference for government's relations to the business cycle.[67]

In the first Washington administration and in nineteenth-century public lands policies the national government used its fiscal
and monetary capacities to channel economic growth into selected sectors of the economy. But the 1930s' programs took responsibility to maintain the basic vitality of the market as a total
institution. In two decisions of high symbolic as well as practical
meaning the Supreme Court underlined this broadening of the
public role. When Congress and the president took the country
off the gold standard and forbade trading in gold, the Court
denied relief to holders of outstanding debt instruments calling

for payment in gold.[68] When the Minnesota legislature imposed a qualified moratorium on foreclosures under existing mortgages, the Court upheld the statute against a contract clause challenge. The Court ruled that the legislature could reasonably find the measure necessary to halt an accelerating decline in land values which put in peril the whole financial structure of the state's economy.[69] The functional significance of the decisions was to validate legislative authority to subordinate the law's normal respect for particular contract obligations to public interest in keeping alive the market context without which all contracts would lose value.[70]

Of broader reach and deeper impact than such retroactive public measures have been the forward-looking uses of law to moderate damaging shifts in the general course of business. Thanks to the Sixteenth Amendment and economic growth, the twentieth-century national government has commanded fiscal resources far beyond those available in the nineteenth century. The 1930s had seen the first major resort to these enhanced taxing and spending capacities to sustain purchasing power in a flagging economy. But the New Deal years were charged with bitter controversy over the basic legitimacy of official intervention to moderate major swings in economic activity. Then, fearing a depression which did not arrive, in the Employment Act of 1946 Congress formally declared it the policy of the United States to use the monetary and fiscal powers of the national government to maintain employment and a vigorous flow of business. Jealous of expanded public roles, business lobbies defeated more ambitious proposals that would have committed government to plan and implement programs for "full" employment. But even in the diluted form in which it passed, the Employment Act of 1946 was a landmark.[71] For all its limited effects, the Sherman Act nonetheless had been of profound significance for recognizing that the national government had a positive responsibility to keep competition alive in the market. Similarly the 1946 act was important for overtly acknowledging positive government responsibility to hold within politically and socially acceptable bounds the costs of deflationary currents in the general economy. From mid-twentieth century, in this domain, argument was on means rather than on the objective. In the 1960s Congress and the president translated this commitment into new styles of tax policy. In 1961 and 1962 Congress provided an investment tax credit and the Treasury liberalized rules governing the depreciation practices of business firms, to encourage business investment. In 1964 Congress passed a tax reduction designed to relieve the drag which increased tax receipts were seen to be putting on promising economic growth.[72] Yet experience of the 1970s taught that we were still a long way from competence to achieve fine adjustments in the economy. Policymakers have continued to be hampered by deficiencies in theory and data. Moreover, if the 1950s and 1960s taught a good deal about using fiscal and monetary policies against deflation, the 1970s have shown that we had yet to learn how to curb the damaging costs of inflation. The 1946 act signalled that the country had put behind it doctrinaire objections to using government against deflation. But hesitant and faltering policy in the 1970s have shown how strong are the political obstacles to effective budget cuts posed by special interests and by broadly held expectations clustered about past public spending.[73] Further, on all fronts the difficulties of successful domestic governance of the economy have been increased in the latter twentieth century by impacts of multinational corporations and of globally linked markets. Policy history in containing large economic movements is still much in the making in the 1980s.

ACCOUNTING FOR GAINS AND COSTS
OTHER THAN BY A MARKET CALCULUS

Working as they usually did by relatively blunt, trial-and-error methods, legal processes did not produce policy that would satisfy sophisticated economic or social analysis. But some main currents of law did move toward supplementing the market calculus with forms of social income and cost accounting embracing wider ranges of factors and longer spans of time. In another perspective these directions of policy sought to achieve more accurate and realistic, because more inclusive, criteria of economic productivity than private market processes provided. Some public programs geared to accounting and productivity concepts beyond those of the market reached back through the nineteenth century to the recommendations of Alexander Hamilton in Washington's first administration. But, as in other aspects of the country's legal history, the most marked and most numerous departures from conventions of market accounting began about the 1880s and gathered force particularly after 1930. We should distinguish these lines of policy from those dealing with problems of mutuality in bargaining, business concentration, and impacts of deflation and inflation. In those areas public policy focused on preserving the private market from tendencies within it threatening its existence. The areas of policy I now sketch lay outside the market, and developed precisely because politically effective opinion saw that there were values important to the quality of people's lives for which the market calculus did not provide.

This perception translated into particularly sharp definition in key decisions of the Supreme Court limiting application of the contract clause and asserting the community's legitimate power to subordinate market-oriented claims to other than market values. In *Providence Bank* v. *Billings* (1830) the Marshall Court refused to imply a tax exemption in a statutory charter; if such an exemption were to exist, it must be by explicit grant. The Chief Justice centered on the fact that, by its function, the tax power was at the heart of government's capacity to provide for needs of the total community, and "as the whole community is interested in retaining it undiminished, that community has a right to insist that its abandonment ought not to be presumed in

a case in which the deliberate purpose of the State to abandon it
does not appear."[74] Market advantages claimed under law must
yield to commonwealth values:

> The power of legislation, and consequently of taxation, operates
> on all the persons and property belonging to the body politic.
> This is an original principle, which has its foundation in society it-
> self. It is granted by all, for the benefit of all. It resides in govern-
> ment as a part of itself, and need not be reserved when property of
> any description, or the right to use it in any manner, is granted to
> individuals or corporate bodies. However absolute the right of an
> individual may be, it is still in the nature of that right that it must
> bear a portion of the public burdens, and that portion must be de-
> termined by the Legislature. This vital power may be abused; but
> the Constitution of the United States was not intended to furnish
> the corrective for every abuse of power which may be committed
> by the State governments. The interest, wisdom, and justice of the
> representative body, and its relations with its constituents furnish
> the only security where there is no express contract against unjust
> and excessive taxation, as well as against unwise legislation gener-
> ally.[75]

In refusing to imply a grant of statutory monopoly to the Proprietors of the Charles River Bridge the Taney Court in 1837
showed that the key issue was whether a claim of law-given market advantage ran against values critical to the general structure
of a well ordered society.

> [I]n a country like ours, free, active, and enterprising, continually
> advancing in numbers and wealth, new channels of communica-
> tion are daily found necessary, both for travel and trade, and are
> essential to the comfort, convenience, and prosperity of the peo-
> ple. A State ought never to be presumed to surrender this power,
> because, like the taxing power, the whole community have an in-
> terest in preserving it undiminished. . . . While the rights of pri-
> vate property are sacredly guarded, we must not forget that the
> community also have rights and that the happiness and well-being
> of every citizen depends on their faithful preservation.[76]

Later decisions amplified the principle thus announced,
though under the less enlightening formula that a state may not

contract away its "police power." Thus *Stone* v. *Mississippi* (1880) ruled that a state constitutional provision and its implementing legislation prohibiting lotteries did not infringe the contract clause, though it defeated a grant of a lottery privilege conferred by an earlier statutory franchise.[77] The legislature holds continuing authority to act in behalf of interests it reasonably finds important to a healthy state of society, and particularly interests not defined simply by transactions for profit in market:

> The contracts which the Constitution protects are those that relate to property rights, not governmental. It is not always easy to tell on which side of the line which separates governmental from property rights a particular case is to be put; but in respect to lotteries there can be no difficulty. . . . They are a species of gambling and wrong in their influences. They disturb the checks and balances of a well ordered community. Society built on such a foundation would almost of necessity bring forth a population of speculators and gamblers. . . . Anyone, therefore, who accepts a lottery charter, does so with the implied understanding that the People, in their sovereign capacity and through their properly constituted agencies, may resume it at any time when the public good shall require, and this whether it be paid for or not.[78]

Similarly, legal charters to conduct industrial operations, such as a slaughtering house or rendering plant, must yield before later reasonable legislative judgment that the growth of the community has made the operations dangerous to public health or safety or intolerable to basic amenities of social living.[79]

Compared with doctrine built under the commerce clause or the due process and equal protection clauses, contract clause litigation does not hold a preeminent position in constitutional history. But these contract clause decisions are peculiarly indicative for the theme of this essay. The aggrieved business firms in such cases were asserting a high claim to legal protection of market values—respect for prior commitments of assets in market made under inducements of law. The Court's rulings thus give specially sharp definition to commonwealth values: lawmakers enjoy broad scope for judgment in subordinating market claims or entitlements to needs of a healthy social context, including values other than those measured in market terms.[80]

The main substance of policy adjusting the market to other elements of social context has been contained, not in judge-made law, but in statute law and administrative rules and orders. Two principal lines of development stand out—one of legal action concerning the direction, scale, and timing of massive allocations of investment capital, the other dealing with social overhead costs of providing and protecting the resource bases of society.

In the ordinary course of affairs capital allocation has been a prime function of the private market. But as early as Hamilton's Report on the Subject of Manufactures (1791) policymakers were not content to stay within the bounds of what the market might be expected to accomplish. Primarily by using government's fiscal powers—which, functionally defined, included disposition of public lands and of publicly granted franchises—they have undertaken to establish some priorities in allocating capital on a scale far exceeding the market's capacities. Thus, Congress disposed of a great part of the public domain by sales to farmers or to speculative developers—and, to a less extent, in exchange for labor in opening acres to cultivation—to promote an economy of commercial agriculture in the Mississippi Valley.[81] The United States and states acting under grants from Congress, used public lands as well as public loans and grants of money to subsidize construction of railroads and canals.[82] Incident to both policies, Congress encouraged private lenders, including speculative investors, to venture money in promoting commercial farming and railroads by making public lands available as eventual backing for mortgage security.[83] From 1816 Congress embarked on a long and controversial course of implementing Hamilton's recommendation of protective tariffs to foster growth of industry. In detail over the years tariff-making became a weapon of special interest maneuver. For most of the nine-teenth and early twentieth centuries, tariff changes probably had only marginal impact on the economy as a whole, however crit-ical they were for particular sectors. But tariff issues loomed large in political combat over proper uses of law as means to channel growth in manufacturing and extractive industries. And tightening international competition in the second half of the twentieth century has made the economic impact issue more real.[84] In the twentieth century, states, and in the later twentieth century, Congress, have subsidized expanded use of automobiles and trucks—to the cost of the railroads—through heavy public spending on hard-surfaced highways. Like the tariff, highway programs have been important, indeed indispensable, supports of many specific market activities, not only of makers of autos and trucks, but also of suppliers and dealers to the industries, and of common carriers, local merchants, and dairy and truck farmers. But public spending on roads has enjoyed a breadth and continuity of political support beyond that which could be cred-ited solely to special interests in the market. As with capital sub-sidies to agriculture and transportation, highway appropriations represent a rudely shaped type of major economic and social plan-ning. It is planning which has pursued goals of general economic and social growth and has responded to broadly shared ideas of the good life. Involved have been ambitions of ordinary people as well as entrepreneurs which called for mustering and channeling assets on a scale beyond what the private market alone could ac-complish.[85] At first under the spur of World War II needs and then of peacetime competition with Russia, in the mid and later twentieth century Congress invested large public monies in real-izing the promise of science-based technology. Public funds have thus directed the energies of the market toward nuclear power, space exploration, and new levels of sophisticated medicine. Eventually these public investments have served developing markets and in some degree market-oriented special interests.

But public commitments to promoting basic research and advanced technology have involved broad concerns for the country's security and economic strength. The governing attitudes have reflected fears of war or domestic unrest and challenges to national pride that have produced political support for assigning capital priorities beyond the market's competence.[86]

For continuity if not also for growth any economy depends on a base of physical, biological, human, and social resources. In some ways in its early years the United States was acutely conscious of problems in its resource base. The country was scarce in human power; it encouraged immigration and under the commerce clause and common law freedom of contract protected free internal movement of people to where they could find work.[87] As legislatures sensed the need of an educated electorate and labor force they slowly built on Jefferson's recommendation to establish public schools.[88] In an economy short of fluid capital, law liberalized availability of the corporation to muster scattered capital.[89] Yet, the nineteenth century was also unaware or heedless of major threats to its resource base. Until the Lake States forest disappeared as a continuing source of lumber, policymakers ritually proclaimed that timberland was inexhaustible.[90] Cities and industrial activity grew apace, tardy in even rudimentary care for public health and safety, and in result suffered recurrent epidemics and inhumane as well as uneconomic costs to the labor force through unsafe and unsanitary working conditions.[91] Of course, the pattern of mingled inertia, naivete, and short-term profit-seeking has not been unknown to the twentieth century. Within freedom of contract in market the explosive introduction of chemicals has revolutionized manufacturing and processing operations in the first half of the century. Public policy has lagged by a generation in awareness that the new techniques call for more sophisticated accounting for the costs as well as gains of the new methods.[92]

After feeble beginnings from about 1880, politically effective opinion slowly gathered momentum toward increased attention to resource-base issues not readily handled through the market. We can bound the change between the improved factory safety laws and workers' compensation acts which went on the books between 1890 and 1920, and the National Environmental Policy Act of 1969.[93] Within that span legislation dealt also with safety of food and drugs.[94] Zoning laws reacted to economic as well as social costs to the quality of urban life from haphazard land use developments; eventually the idea of zoning was extended to rural areas.[95] Air and water pollution became subjects of statutory and administrative regulation.[96] In the second half of the twentieth century worry over the quality of schooling as well as racial and religious tensions involving the schools have prompted fresh attention to choices people must make in financing and programming education.[97] Racial, ethnic, and sex tensions have been thrust into markets for jobs and housing. Circumstances thus have pressed lawmakers to deal with challenges to social peace to which the market's usual acceptance of the status quo is not responsive.[98]

There has also been broader attention to adjusting the market to the needs of the society's total resource base. Public policy has advanced toward a more realistic, if not always sophisticated, appreciation that the market depends on a healthy social context. In more inclusive ways than those envisaged in John Locke's emphasis on commonwealth or in Henry George's analysis of *Progress and Poverty,* twentieth-century public policy is realizing the social bases of productivity. New lines of policy in effect acknowledge that economic productivity derives not simply from the private market but also from opportunities and efficiencies created by the total terms on which people succeed in living together.[99] On the negative side, the law's new-found care for the whole resource base has expressed dissatisfaction with limits that inhere in private market processes—the narrow focus of such dealings on goals of the immediate bargainers and on interests readily measured in money; the bias toward potent change worked in the immediate present by increments too often unnoticed in their long-term, broad-scale impacts; and the typically unexamined acceptance of a given distribution of wealth, income, and social and political power. These negative aspects of market processes have been the reverse side of positive strengths. A prime challenge to legal processes in the late twentieth century is to reach adjustments which will usefully supplement the market without wastefully displacing it as a component of social order.

CHAPTER 3

Bargaining through Law and through Markets

Ours has been an energetic society in which individuals and groups have sought on many fronts to use law to manage what went on. We have enjoyed large freedom from earlier, established structures of power and order. No established, indigenous culture was strong enough to impose its ways on newcomers. Both abundance of land and timing of settlement precluded the creation of a feudal order that would fix everyone in an appointed place. As with all communities, customs existed and grew to channel particular ways of dealing. But from the seventeenth through much of the nineteenth century the limited means with which individuals and groups confronted a raw continent put a premium on improvisation and contrivance which displaced custom from a central role in ordering affairs. The break with the Empire required unusual attention to restructuring the legal order, first through the state constitutions and the Federal Constitution, then through state and national legislation and common law directed at organizing government agencies and providing a body of doctrines adapted to domestic private and public business. These were prime moving factors particularly from the 1770s through the first quarter of the nineteenth century. From about the 1830s a powerful new element entered, as changing technology—and later, science-based technology—increased the intricacy of the division of labor, the interlock of social processes, and the interdependence of people, all to the result of emphasizing needs for more deliberate arrangement of social relations.

For wide-reaching, conscious contrivance of social structure and processes this society relied more on law and the market than on any other institutions. However important, other institutions operated within more confined bounds. The family ordered close, small-group dealings. The church centered on individual emotional response to life and on close personal relations; usually it undertook to muster its members for community action only within a limited range of issues. Schools pursued the important but specialized functions of helping induct the young into the patterns of their elders; from about mid-nineteenth century, the more people saw educators' task as directly affecting social order, the more formal education became primarily a governmental function and a part of legal process. The growth of private, secular associations operating for other than market purposes early became a major element in social organization; Tocqueville observed this development in full vigor in the 1830s. Most private associations, however, focused on limited goals or fields of interest. Their broadest reach into the general community was likely to consist in their involvement with legal processes, as they sought to lobby for or against law's involvement with their immediate concerns.

Two aspects of the country's experience seem specially to account for the preeminent roles of legal and market processes in adjusting social relations. (1) The scale, complexity, and interdependence of social operations steadily multiplied. This growth called for increasing investments of human effort and economic assets both in market and in other than market facilities to sustain the common life. The course of affairs put premiums on institutions capable of mustering potent collective effort. By the late eighteenth century the inheritance of institutional capacities with which law was endowed in the Anglo-American tradition gave legal processes great potential for collective effort. In less obvious because less direct ways the market as it developed from the late eighteenth into the late nineteenth century had similar utility. From an early stage, the market provided patterns of behavior for bringing to a focus otherwise scattered energies and assets. Later, helped by developments in law and in technology, the market afforded leverage for novel degrees of concentration of private decisionmaking capacity. (2) A second feature of the country's growth thrust law and the market to the fore. This was the development of a great diversity of interests and functions, fostered by the growth of a population working upon a rich and manifold natural resource base, moved by the restless ambitions of a rising-middle-class outlook on life, and impelled by technological and scientific advances into headlong change and expansion of options for employing individual and group capacities. A society of this character needed institutions equipped to deal with wide ranges of ends and means and to respond flexibly to change and to competition among different wants and needs. For the law, the legislative branch especially had such potential. For its part, encouraged by legal freedom of contract and protection of property, the market provided a broad arena of maneuver for bargainers, welcoming accommodation of a great range, volume, and variety of transactions and enterprises.

COMMAND AND AGREEMENT, MONOPOLY AND COMPETITION, AND THE CONSTITUTIONAL IDEAL

In origins, purposes, and methods legal processes and market processes have been substantially distinct and different ways of adjusting relations in society. But in operation the two have been less far apart than their formal aspects indicated. Both their contrasts and their resemblances have materially affected the social history of law. Two pairs of features stand out: the law as an area of commands, the market as an area of agreements; and the law as a monopoly of services and regulations, the market as a regime of competition.

The most distinctive feature of the legal system has been its continuing claim to possess and use the legitimate monopoly of physical force to impose values and employ means to effect them. The central place and reality of this claim stood attested by the revolution which separated the colonies from the Empire, by the creation of the state and federal constitutions, and by the continuing emphasis which the criminal law gave to punishing unauthorized use of private force to pursue group objectives.[1] Usually the element of official force has been in the background, especially where legal agencies have conferred special privileges under law (franchises) or provided such services as roads and schools. Yet the government's force has also underwritten franchises and services. Back of public schools and public welfare institutions stands the tax collector, and back of him, the sheriff or ultimately the militia.[2] A franchise gives to particular individuals or groups privileges to act, or to be free of official restraints on action, in ways denied the general run of people. Back of such a franchise stands the law's capacity to interfere if it has not given its permission. The law did not compel promoters of a turnpike, railroad, or toll bridge to build their facility. But if they bridged a navigable stream without the law's permission, courts would enjoin their operation and punish them for creating a public nuisance; and if they tried to buy a right-of-way for a turnpike or railroad, they were likely to be balked by hold-out private landowners unless government lent them its power to take private property for a public purpose on payment fixed by legal proceedings.[3]

In contrast to law, market processes commonly operate by agreement to reach adjustments of relations on terms workably satisfying to those involved. Such has been both the common perception and in large measure the working reality of the market. Prime evidence of the image and the reality lies in growth and continuity of the volume of transactions initiated and carried out by private actors without official intervention.[4] The law's specialized attention to prices and terms of service in limited areas historically marked out as public utilities testifies how far the assumed norm has been that private agreement would structure most private exchanges.[5] The law presumes that private contracts reflect true agreements among the parties, and the burden is on one who would avoid his apparent obligation to show defenses of duress, fraud, or basic mistake of fact.[6] Common law and later statutory and administrative redress against forms of unfair competition have condemned conduct which subverts the norm of free private agreements, as by wrongful intimidation of potential traders, or resort to bribery or espionage directed at a competitor's business organization, or use of fraud or deceit to entice customers away from honest dealers.[7]

The second contrast between legal processes and market processes for adjusting relationships has been that between monopoly and competition. Typically, legal processes offer services which only official agencies provide, or which only official agencies provide on terms which tend to bring to them the greatest number of recipients. Or legal processes regulate behavior for purposes and by means which only official agencies define and implement under sanctions of constitutionally authorized compulsion. In part, the monopoly characteristic of law rests on the law's successful assertion that law holds the legitimate monopoly of physical force. In part, the monopoly rests on the fact that the nature of certain goods which people want or enjoy require assembling economic resources and types of arrangements beyond the capacities of even large-scale private organizations. In part it rests on the fact that certain utilities or values are so diffuse in impact that private transactions for profit cannot capture them to allocate their costs and benefits.[8]

For various reasons, therefore, legal processes, whether for service or regulation, more often than not have held a monopoly in their fields of operation. This has not been the condition of all aspects of legal order as it has developed in the United States. But it has marked more legal operations than it has excluded. In various aspects law has reflected the reality of this monopoly character. For example, a good deal of the criminal law has been auxiliary to the integrity of the market and hence has been directed largely to assisting procedures for achieving agreement among individuals and groups. But of equal emphasis in the statute books have been laws defining crimes of violence or threatened violence against the state and against the person, focused thus on conduct immediately threatening the state's legitimate monopoly of force.[9] On the civil side, the law of franchises has clearly presented the law as a monopoly; only the state may authorize private action that entails special legal privileges, such as charging tolls for using a bridge, or taking land by delegated eminent domain power, or damming a navigable stream to develop power to turn grist mills or electric generators.[10]

In contrast to the monopoly element in law, the ideal of market processes has been to work through different sources for offering or obtaining goods or services. Monopoly is the opposite of what the community wants when it values the market as an institution for promoting efficient allocation of resources. From the late eighteenth century through much of the nineteenth, practice typically matched the model of the market. Explosive nineteenth-century growth in numbers of traders and transactions emphasized the interaction of many actors in the play of supply and demand. So far as they fulfilled the ideal of the market these actors enjoyed a wide enough range of options to introduce considerable play in the economy.[11] Nineteenth-century public policy reflected and fostered this competitive model through its favor for broad legal freedom of private contract; late-nineteenth- and twentieth-century policy added the element of positive government responsibility through the antitrust laws specifically to ban monopoly and to keep alive and vigorous a diversity of bargainers in private arenas.[12]

Experience with government and with the market has taught that both institutions have provided leverage by which some individuals or groups can exert practical as well as legal compulsion on the wills of others. From the late eighteenth century on the impacts of power relationships brought into play powerful attitudes and values that imposed themselves on government and the market alike, though through different channels. These values and attitudes shaped the idea and the ideal of constitutionalism—that in a humane society, there should be no centers of unchecked practical or legal power of some people over others. Every center of legal or practical power should be subject in material degree to checks exercised from outside itself, regarding the ends it pursued and the means by which it pursued them. The idea and the ideal have had long, complex histories. They have derived in part from religious insistence on the intrinsic worth and dignity of individuals, in part from political experience in evolving representative government, in part from energies released by growth of markets, in part from increased rationalization of the economy spurred by advances in technology and science which in turn have called for rationality in using law. Legal processes and market processes have contributed to the emergence of the idea and the ideal of constitutionalism, but the idea and the ideal in turn have exercised substantial effect in shaping law and the market.[13]

Constitutionalism has two components, one of deeper value than the other. One requirement for legitimizing practical or legal power is that power be used rationally, that is, that power-holders choose at least their intermediate goals by reasoned examination of relevant facts and values, and choose means reasonably calculated to reach their goals. In this aspect constitutionalism expresses the bias of this culture for efficient use of resources.[14] But rationality has not been enough; policymakers can adopt rational programs to reach indecent ends. A deeper demand has been that organization for holding and using power be consistent with humane regard for the worth and dignity of individuals living within the power system, and that the objectives of using power be consistent with the same criterion of ultimate regard for the quality of individual life. In this aspect the idea and the ideal of constitutionalism have added demands of humanity to those of rational efficiency.[15]

The two aspects of contrast between legal processes and market processes relate to the two different levels of the constitutional idea and ideal. The general contrast between the law's reliance on command and the market's reliance on agreement emphasizes differences in procedures by which the two institutions undertook to fulfill their social functions. What developed in this domain was primarily a search for rational efficiency in relating means to ends; command was generally justified so far as it produced desired results where reliance on private agreement would not; the efficiency of private agreement was generally justified insofar as it realistically expressed accommodation of differing wants, and was not merely a cloak for compulsion.[16] On the other hand, the general contrast between the law's focus on criteria of political legitimacy to warrant its monopoly of force and the market's reliance on interplay of diverse sources of supply or demand pointed to the deeper requirement, that powerholding and its use be consistent with respect for the humane quality of life.[17] Under both heads of constitutionalism— the demand for rational efficiency and the demand for respect for human values—the country's experience produced blurrings of the general distinctions between law and the market. Each institution tended to take on some degree of the distinguishing characteristics of the other. These shifts in some ways helped realize the constitutional idea and in some ways created problems for it.

LEGITIMACY CONFERRED BY EFFICIENCY: MERGER OF CHARACTERISTICS OF LAW AND THE MARKET

Experience demonstrated that law was not effective—that is, did not meet the requirement of rational efficiency under constitutionalism—simply by command. Nor did the market operate simply through private agreements among freely bargaining parties. In practice each institution gained continuity and impact largely through working characteristics similar to those of the other. In time politically effective opinion accepted or at least acquiesced in many of these developments.

In their actions most of the time lawmakers showed that they realized that the law's force was normally effective only if it played a marginal role in making and effecting public policy.[18] Effectiveness was not the whole of the matter. The Anglo-American constitutional tradition, classically crystallized by Locke, assigned high substantive value to holding law to the sphere of "public" interests and protecting individuals in substantial areas of their "private" affairs; the qualified legal autonomy of the market was a salient element of that constitutional value. Yet the limits which practice put on resort to law also had grounding in considerations of what would work.[19] The breakdown of the Union in sectional war in 1861 dramatized the problem of the limits of effective legal action. It was a challenge which conflicting interests rarely brought to such a tragic outcome, and which therefore was not usually to the fore of public attention. In less extreme degree and in varying ways nineteenth- and twentieth-century use of government's taxing and spending powers involved the issue. Of course, that law typically was a marginal force in shaping social experience was not simply the product of conscious policy. The limits of people's knowledge, energies, and courage as they confronted the total press of experience, and the narrow pragmatism of a culture habituated to seeking immediate, tangible returns for effort, were factors of context which subtly but powerfully constricted resort to the law's force and contrivances.[20] Nonetheless, the course of public policy also reflected considerable awareness of the limits of effective legal action.[21]

Command was the emphasis in the new national government's response in 1794 to the collective, sometimes violent defiance offered by western Pennsylvania farmers to paying a federal excise on whiskey.[22] Secretary of the Treasury Hamilton felt keenly the uncertain status of national authority following the battles fought over ratifying the Constitution and over the fiscal and monetary programs he led to enactment in Washington's first administration. Convinced that the national government should play a vigorous role in promoting growth in key areas of the economy, Hamilton was not only concerned by the farmers' challenge, but also eager to set an early, decisive precedent for obedience to the new government's laws. President Washington shared his secretary's judgment that the United States must demonstrate its capacity to govern. On Hamilton's advice the president mustered an army of over 12,000 men before which the Pennsylvanians' resistance quickly crumbled. The experience pointed up two propositions. First, Hamilton got his desired precedent for the law's successful assertion that it held the legitimate monopoly of force. There were two important corollaries here. Having determined to use force, government had acted wisely by invoking it on such a scale as to overwhelm opposition. Then, having made the point, the president was prudently restrained in the aftermath; two leaders of the disturbance were convicted of treason by levying war, but were later pardoned.[23] The second lesson implicit in the Whiskey Rebellion bore on the limits of effective legal action. Practical-minded lawmakers could not overlook a caution implicit in the affair. The Pennsylvania tumult showed that it was politically risky in a cash-scarce economy for government to depend any more than it had to upon the obvious exactions of the tax collector.[24] Looking back to the formative years of Wisconsin, Justice Roujet Marshall, speaking for the Wisconsin Supreme Court, observed that "in the early days of the commonwealth when everything was in a primitive state, burdens of taxation to care for the real necessities of civil government were all that could be borne."[25] The Wisconsin constitution of 1848 reflected this temper of the times in the cumulative limits it put on public spending. Taxes must be uniform; the legislature must make only specific appropriations for specified purposes; the state might not lend its credit or contract debt beyond closely defined limits; each legislative chamber must take a yea and nay vote on all fiscal measures, subject to a special quorum requirement that three-fourths of the members be present in each house; the state might issue no evidences of debt except in the most narrowly defined emergency; the state might not be a party to works of internal improvement. "Could a more closely fenced in field be thought of?" asked Marshall, "leaving nothing therein but ordinary and necessary matters of civil government?"[26] Marshall used his appraisal of the past as a basis for imposing narrow limits on the purposes for which the legislature might use its fiscal powers. The argument lacked warrant, since, except for the ban on state involvement in internal improvements, all the provisions he invoked were limits on the procedures and not on the objectives of legislative fiscal policy.[27] As an estimate of history, however, Marshall's was a correct statement of the prevailing mid-nineteenth-century awareness of the constraints which a cash-scarce economy imposed on public action.

Prudent reluctance to rely heavily on the tax collector had a counterpart in early stages of state law on corporations and special-privilege franchises. Long before legislatures began commonly to provide general acts for incorporation of business enterprises—indeed, during years in which legislatures viewed with distrust the availability of the corporate device for business purposes—legislators passed general acts for incorporating various types of collective, philanthropic undertakings, such as hospitals, libraries, and schools. Communities needed general-service, nonprofit facilities to educate the young and to care for sick and dependent individuals. In the relatively rude condition of the typical state economy it was administratively impracticable—and, the Whiskey Rebellion attested, possibly politically hazardous—to try to meet such public needs by spending tax-derived money. Thus, from the late eighteenth century well into the middle nineteenth, states offered a legal facility, the eleemosynary corporation, to encourage mustering capital by private, cooperative effort, minimizing the presence of the tax collector's com-

pulsion. In such corporate charters legislatures at once legitimized enterprises deemed of public interest and sought to meet
public needs by relying on private agreement.[28] In the *Dartmouth College Case* the United States Supreme Court cast the
protection of the national Constitution's contract clause about
the charter of such a philanthropic institution. Chief Justice
Marshall in effect conceded that the Court was extending the
contract clause beyond the likely focus of the framers—which
had been to bar retroactive state laws relieving distressed debtors
of the full enforcement of rights of their creditors under private
bargains previously struck. Some strongly felt policies moved the
Court so to enlarge the contract clause. One salient goal, Marshall noted, was to maintain the efficacy of the technique of
enlisting volunteer effort to serve public interest: "The objects
for which a corporation is created are universally such as the
government wishes to promote. They are deemed beneficial to
the country; and this benefit constitutes the consideration of the
grant, in most cases, the sole consideration of the grant. In most
eleemosynary institutions, the object would be difficult, perhaps
unattainable without the aid of a charter of incorporation. . . .
These eleemosynary institutions do not fill the place which
would otherwise be occupied by government, but that which
would otherwise remain vacant."[29]

Pursuing an analogous line of policy, nineteenth-century legislatures granted franchises to private promoters to provide public
transport facilities. Public money built some canals, though the
high success of the Erie Canal proved misleading; many such
public undertakings failed or had only indifferent success.[30]
Most often lawmakers relied on devices to muster private capital
to meet transport needs. Where railroads were involved, the
hope of substantial profit impelled private effort. There also,
however, problems of a cash-scarce economy affected use of
legal processes; government gave subsidies in kind by grants of
public lands for right-of-way or to equip promoters with security
they could mortgage to investment bankers; government helped
further by delegating its power of eminent domain to the rail-

road builders so that they might fend off exorbitant demands by hold-out landowners.[31] In addition to railroads, there were two kinds of transportation facility improvements highly important to local economic development—turnpike construction and navigation aids. Again, by granting franchises conferring rights-of-way and privileges of altering natural stream flow, lawmakers enlisted private effort to meet public needs. Typically, turnpike or navigation improvement schemes conferred rights to charge tolls. Thus, such undertakings might seem to belong to the general category of profit-seeking market ventures. However, the profits were probably not of such size as to explain the ventures; functionally, these highway or river improvements principally served the need of local economies for low-return, overhead capital beneficial much more to other activities dependent on the facilities than to the immediate gain of the providers. In substance, thus, resort to franchises for toll roads and stream improvements was close to the grant of corporate charters to sponsors of libraries, schools, or hospitals. Nineteenth-century government was minimizing the compulsions of the tax collector by rallying private, volunteer effort to do what twentieth-century government would do by spending tax-derived money.[32]

In the twentieth century, in a high-production economy now ready with fluid resources, taxation—especially the income tax—yielded means by which government could act directly on far wider fronts than in the nineteenth century. Yet, even so, prudence continued to dictate promoting volunteer efforts to pursue public policy ends. Now, however, a prime instrument to this purpose was the tax structure itself. Resort to the income tax invited legislative flexibility in defining taxable income. Policymakers learned that definitions of taxable income could serve substantive policy goals other than raising revenue. Thus, in a fashion not without analogy to the technique Marshall praised in the *Dartmouth College Case,* Congress encouraged public-interest, philanthropic enterprises by allowing individual and corporate taxpayers to deduct charitable contributions from otherwise taxable income. To foster private investment in plant and equipment Congress allowed deduction of charges to build depreciation reserves and manipulated depreciation formulas as tools of economic planning. In the 1980s, given new concern with energy costs and shortages, legislators allowed taxpayers deductions for weatherstripping or insulating their houses or adding fuel-saving devices to their furnaces. Conceivably Congress could mandate much of this behavior, directly by regulation or indirectly by subsidies from tax-derived funds. But mandates would rouse predictable political controversy. Certainly experience showed that they would rouse controversy beyond any likely to be stirred by combining the background threat of the tax collector with invitations to taxpayers to cooperate by accepting opportunities to take tax deductions or credits.[33]

Legislation was not the only area in which officials and private individuals and groups reduced the level of law's commands by mingling compulsion with agreement. Data are lacking to measure nineteenth-century movements of executive, administrative, or judicial action. Twentieth-century evidence is more available, to show how far legal processes merged command and agreement. Plea bargaining disposed of the bulk of criminal prosecutions. Consent decrees frequently resolved government's antitrust proceedings. The bulk of private lawsuits over breach of contract or personal injury did not reach disposition in court on the merits, but ended by bargained, out-of-court settlements. In analogous fashion, consent orders or agreed determinations ended many enforcement proceedings before administrative agencies. A greater volume of matters brought to law in the twentieth century increased practical inducements to such dispositions short of formal resort to the law's full sanctions. But it seems plausible that similar inducements also operated in the nineteenth century. The persistent mingling of command and agreement in operations of legal processes underlined the fact that law's force was normally a marginal, or at least indirect, factor in determining the working content of public policy.[34]

As experience taught that the law did not rely simply on compulsion, so it taught, also, that the market did not function simply by agreement. Inequality of practical power among particular parties to particular contracts was a familiar fact of life, but a fact which could coexist with general patterns of free give-and-take among large numbers of bargainers. The character of the market substantially altered when and insofar as the structure of relations among broad classes of bargainers put those on one side of the table regularly at a disadvantage relative to those on the other side. Such developments grew out of major changes in organizing production and distribution of goods and services. Shifts of this kind introduced large elements of command into what were in form relations fixed by agreement.

A prime nineteenth-century example of continuing positions of superiority and subordination was the relation between mortgagors and mortgagees of farmland, much colored by division between sources of investment capital in the more settled East and demands for investment capital in the newly opened West. Establishing a farm in the unsettled lands west of the Appalachians called for more cash capital than most settlers could provide. To some extent national and state policies regarding disposition of the public domain responded to the situation in a way which fit the general pattern of reducing the direct impact of the law's compulsion. The United States—and states insofar as grants of land to them from Congress delegated policy to them—made land available to settlers or to speculative developers at prices relatively low compared with the potential value of the land once it was cleared and put under cultivation. These prices in effect subsidized entry of private lenders into the market for farm debt, by leaving an attractive cushion of security for the private mortgagee. Once farms were established, they often stayed in operation subject to continued borrowing from banks and merchants, secured by liens on growing crops. Overall, in the span of two generations the combination of public lands policy and private lending worked to create a broad-scale commercial agriculture in the Mississippi Valley; analogous, though somewhat different, patterns prevailed in expanding plantation production in the South and near Southwest.[35] Out of these events emerged a characteristic tension of creditor and debtor interests which accounted more than any other single factor for the course of public controversy over relations of law and the market into the 1870s. The realities of the tension were implied early on the creditor side, first in the Northwest Ordinance and then in the Constitution, in the inclusion of a clause protecting contracts against retroactive state legislation which would impair the obligation of contracts.[36] The other side of this policy history included statutes against usurious interest, and recurrent legislation imposing moratoria on mortgage foreclosures in times of general economic distress.[37] Reactions to creditor-debtor relations in agricultural areas were factors, also, in the controversy over the rechartering of the Second Bank of the United States, as well as in the late-nineteenth-century battles of Populists and silver Democrats for government expansion of the money supply.[38] This long, involved chain of policy conflict attested the felt presence of structures of command which materially qualified the course of market bargaining.

In the last half of the nineteenth century the structure of industry, commerce, and finance changed rapidly in ways which tended to substitute hierarchy for trade in private allocation of resources. Beginning with the railroads, new technologies required larger concentration of capital and fostered more sophisticated organization, while growth of population and wealth with improved communications expanded markets. In response, entrepreneurs of high talent—notably, Rockefeller, Carnegie, and Morgan—developed techniques of management which supported operations of unprecedented scale and intricacy.[39] Within this setting markets moved away from older patterns of atomized transactions among many dealers of approximately similar means, to trade overshadowed by relatively small numbers of big firms. Common law favor for freedom of contract and constitutional protection of commerce that reached out for sectional or national fields of operation, and the shelters of protective tariffs, invited the new forces to realize their potential.[40]

In the more highly organized economy that emerged from the 1880s many relationships that once would have been bargained out in detail became governed by rank and discipline or by standardized rules laid down at some private center of decision, or by a financial plan devised at some entrepreneurial headquarters. Community practice and law joined to ratify large parts of the new dispensation. Operation of heavy industry required discipline to coordinate and maintain great capital investments and a high division of labor. Shopworkers punched time clocks and followed instructions of foremen, while foremen followed instructions of the front office. In the mid-twentieth century legal regulation of collective bargaining legitimized, while it regulated, patterns of workplace order and command relationships.[41] As business firms have enlarged and integrated stages of production and distribution, functions once performed by independent contractors and subcontractors have become functions of units and divisions of a single enterprise according to budgets, schedules, and plans set by top management.[42] Where linked businesses continue in some bargaining relation to a supplier or customer, the relation is now often governed by private franchises the terms of which are chiefly set by the principal concern; when in the late twentieth century legislatures have imposed some standards of fair dealing on franchisers toward their franchise holders, the presence of the regulations has implied both practical and legal acceptance of substantial relations of superiority and subordination.[43] In close-held firms financing has continued to be a matter of particularized dealing. But in floating large-scale corporate securities issues, bargaining has stayed at the level of top management, its investment bankers and advisers, and institutional investors; for the individual owner of capital, investment has become a matter of buying stocks or bonds on detailed terms fixed by these centralized decisionmakers, subject to some regulations set by government.[44] In the mid-twentieth century, the ultimate consumers of goods and services provided by large enterprises typically exercise initiative only in the decision to enter a relationship whose specifications are set in standard molds by the big firms; the standardized contract has become the norm especially in extending credit and providing security. Standardization can be efficient, saving time and misunderstandings in bargaining and in administering firms, and in adapting terms of trade to the character of particular lines of business. Yet standardization may also involve one party's imposing its discipline or its interests on those on the other side of the deal.[45] Among large firms, antitrust laws bar overt treaties to eliminate or reduce variations in terms of trade. But in markets in which a few big operators do the bulk of business, each firm is likely to make its decisions with a close eye on how its fellows price, advertise, or merchandise their goods. Competition through price or other techniques continues to be a lively factor in most such arenas. Nonetheless, command of major market shares by a relatively few participants means that a kind of informal discipline is likely to prevail much of the time at these rarified altitudes.[46] The widely felt presence of these various types of directed orders raises issues of legitimacy at the deeper level of the constitutional idea. But viewed at the level of working efficiency, these kinds of arrangements or relationships as they have unfolded since the 1880s became accepted, familiar constituents of principal markets; in these markets, at least as many who took part marched under orders as contrived their relations by particularly bargained-out agreements.

LEGITIMACY CONFERRED BY SERVICE
TO HUMANE LIFE IN SOCIETY

The constitutional idea demands that both public and private centers of decision with legal or practical power to compel the will of others should in some sense serve general and not only narrowly focused private interests. Especially should such powerholders be under some effective constraint not to use their positions primarily to serve their own advantage. To that end this tradition insists that relations be so organized that powerholders be subject to checks external to their immediate circle. It is on this issue—not of the efficiency, but of the goals of institutionalized power—that the contrast between situations of monopoly and of competition has produced the most distinctive policies concerning the moral and political legitimacy of legal and market processes.

Different currents have produced policies of accountability for official power and for market power. But in the outcome there is striking similarity between the two lines of policy. Both rely on two interrelated kinds of legal arrangements—those calculated to promote diversity of centers of will for action, and those encouraging competition among such centers.

In the matter of diversity the likeness between policies affecting the law and those affecting the market emerged in a classic episode in the development of the Anglo-American constitutional idea. This was the 1647 debate between the conservative wing of Cromwell's army and the liberal wing, which included the group known as Levellers. Both sides wanted a broader dispersion of political power in England as against the prerogative authority which the Stuarts sought to enlarge and consolidate in the Crown. For the conservatives Ireton—Cromwell's son-in-law and chief of cavalry—advocated government by voters, but voters limited to men of substantial property in freehold estates in land or in membership in municipal corporations. For the liberals Rainborough advocated a suffrage still of limited scope—excluding wage earners and alms takers (as persons lacking means for independent will), and implicitly excluding women—but still a suffrage of greater reach than Ireton's formula would allow. Dispersion of power to determine government's legitimacy was their common emphasis, however, as Ireton sternly admonished his Leveller opponents when he reminded them: "I [will] tell you what the soldier of the kingdom [of Cromwell's army] hath fought for. First, the danger that he stood in was that one man's will must be law. The people of the kingdom must have this right at least, that they should not be concluded [but] by the representative of those that had the interest of the kingdom."[47]

Dispersion of power was as much to the fore in the Levellers' argument for a more extended suffrage. To them the proved danger was that tightly concentrated political power—even power of freeholders and town merchants outside the circle of the Crown—would be used by its holders to oppress those excluded from it. Without broader access to the vote, Rainborough asked, "what the soldier hath fought for all this while?" and answered bitterly, "He hath fought to enslave himself, to give power to men of riches, men of estates, to make him a perpetual slave. We do find in all presses that go forth none must be pressed that are freehold men. When these gentlemen fall out among themselves, they shall press the poor scrubs to come and kill [one another] for them."[48]

For the conservatives Ireton had a positive answer to Rainborough's fears of oppressive power. Ireton's response relied on linking the constitution of government to the constitution of the market. To him the resulting relation would legitimize the total structure of power created by the interplay of the two institutions. Ireton would limit the vote to freeholders and the leading merchants or master craftsmen who were members of municipal corporations, because their wealth gave them a "stake" in social order which assured that they would use the suffrage responsibly. In contrast, he feared, voters lacking substantial property would use the ballot to take the property of those better off. Assets acquired through productive activity in market qualified the holders to share political power and at the same time provided the base from which to break old, oppressive monopolies of power. With the prudent avoidance of extremes characteristic of the rising middle class, however, Ireton stipulated that he did not stand for a closed society. The legal order should be such as to assure that "[m]en may justly have by birthright, by their very being born in England, that we should not seclude them out of England, that we should not refuse to give them air and place and ground, and the freedom of the highways and other things to live among us," though they did not own the property that would qualify them to vote. Ireton was in effect speaking on behalf of legal freedom of contract. That freedom would keep the door open to entry into the ranks of voters of those who by their activity in market might gain the wealth to admit them to the suffrage. For "[e]very man that was born [in the country, that] is a denizen in it, that hath a freedom, he was capable of trading to get money, to get estates by."[49]

Dispersion of decisionmaking centers was closely related to rivalry among centers to protect the constitutional ideal. In the domain of the market, the model to legitimize private power-holding was the existence of vigorous competition. Rapid concentration of capital from the 1880s brought this rationale under severe challenge. The response was to develop federal antitrust policy. The response has been slow, poorly implemented, and attacked as either a charade or as ineffective. But for all its uncertainties, antitrust policy has institutionalized the competitive model as the means for holding market power within the constitutional ideal. In effect Anglo-American tradition has also relied on the competitive model to legitimize official power. But the ways taken to this end have been more varied than those which sought to legitimize power in the private market.

Developments favorable to competitive rivalry to check official power have involved both government agencies and sources of initiative outside government. Government inherently has tended to bring the constitutional ideal under strain because in any given area of public policy there usually has been a high degree of monopoly of practical as well as of legal power. Official activity directed at a particular goal is typically in the first instance the prerogative of some one legal agency. Usually the situation does not involve different agencies contending to establish which will do a given job; there is ordinarily no sanctioned counterpart of competition among suppliers in the private market. Both law and practice, however, have built into the legal order diversity of sources of action, not simply to open legal order to a wider range of contacts with community life, but also to provide analogies to the legitimizing role of competition in the market setting. There have been changes and adaptations over time. Nonetheless, cultivation of this competitive analogy has proved to be a stable element of public policy.

Within official structures pursuit of analogies to the legitimizing role of market competition has centered on the vote, the separation of agencies, and federalism.

No trend of policy has been more consistent over the nation's history than expansion of the suffrage. At the outset states commonly set property qualifications for the vote. But rapid expansion of private, fee simple ownership of land, fostered by national policy in disposing of the public domain, eroded the significance of these limits. Symbolic was the defeat in the New York constitutional convention of 1821 of Chancellor Kent's effort to retain a property qualification at least in election of the second chamber of the state legislature.[50] The North's victory in the Civil War brought the Fifteenth Amendment's formal outlawry of racial criteria for access to the ballot. Though it took a century for the nation to put effective force behind this principle, the 1960's civil rights legislation finally reinforced the long-term pattern of policy.[51] In 1920 the Nineteenth Amendment removed sex barriers to voting, completing a policy which laws of some states had earlier set in motion.[52] In 1966 the United States Supreme Court underlined the eventual victory of Rainborough over Ireton by ruling that the Federal Constitution forbade states to make payment of a tax a condition of the right to vote.[53] Over the years the percentage of eligible voters who went to the polls varied a good deal from one time to another, and from one type of election to another; in the late twentieth century the percent-age of those voting has declined to a troubling extent.[54] How-ever, these ups and downs did not negate the basic significance of the broader suffrage. Wherever there was an electorate of sub-stantial size, the ballot process kept contingent the authority of prime policymakers at all levels of elected government; if tempted to arrogance, officials could not afford to ignore the possibility that voters might dispossess them.[55] Nor was the con-tingency of power the only product of the electoral machinery. From the precedent set under the tensions that surrounded the succession of Thomas Jefferson to John Adams, the ballot pro-cess worked to provide a regularized, peaceful means for trans-ferring authority from one set of official powerholders to an-other. The tragic exception of the Civil War highlighted the sig-nificance of the general pattern, as did contrasts with political turbulence in nineteenth- and twentieth-century autocratic or to-talitarian regimes abroad.[56] Finally, the availability of the ballot process has legitimated a broad arena for peaceful competition of private interests seeking aid or protection from official power. Thus, the vote has opened government to wider and often more changeful arrays of wants and needs than those with which a given body of powerholders might be familiar and comfort-able.[57]

First the new state constitutions and then the national Consti-tution shared lawmaking among separate legal agencies. The prime purpose of this structuring was neither economy nor con-cord. Rather, Justice Brandeis pointed out, "[t]he doctrine of the separation of powers was adopted by the convention of 1787 not to promote efficiency but to preclude the exercise of ar-bitrary power. The purpose was not to avoid friction, but, by means of the inevitable friction incident to the distribution of the governmental powers among three departments, to save the people from autocracy."[58] The roles of the major legal agencies interwove and overlapped to an extent that gave affected in-terests inside and outside official circles various avenues for advancing their programs or bargaining out accommodations. The legislature was central. More and more over the years statute law provided the foundations of public policy, so that by the twentieth century executive and administrative officers and judges generally depended on the legislature to define their missions and arm them with means to do their jobs.[59] Statutes did not execute themselves, however, nor could legislators forecast and control in detail the full variety of situations to which their acts might apply. Thus, the practical impact of legislation continued to be much subject to values and policy attitudes held by lawyers advising private clients and by executive and administrative officials, the bulk of whose actions came under no regular, continuing external review. Time and again the reality was that the particularized development or application of public policy had the character of a monopoly in the hands of particular wielders of power.[60] This is a fact which has always fit uncomfortably with the constitutional ideal. It is a fact which has created a peculiarly important role for courts in providing legitimizing checks on the monopoly-like authority exercised by other lawmakers in specific areas of policy. As events unfolded, the norm of our legal order accorded judges the determining word in particular controversies in interpreting constitutional or statutory language.[61] Practice established the legitimacy of judicial review of the constitutionality of legislation, though only a small proportion of statute law has ever come under such challenge.[62] Of much more frequent impact has been the role of judges in deciding whether executive or administrative action has exceeded the authority which legislators intended to confer on such agencies.[63] There are, however, substantial doctrinal and practical limits on what judges may do. Judges have expressed the felt need of workable comity among agencies in the presumption of constitutionality which they have usually applied to statutes or to delegated legislation regulating the market, and in the weight they have given to continued, consistent executive or administrative practice in construing governing statutes.[64]

Moreover, litigation has its practical limits. Lawsuits are expensive and require more energy, courage, and persistence than many complainants can muster. Too, a given suit focuses on particular grievances, with no firm assurance that the outcome will control what officials do in other instances.[65] Nonetheless, for all the limitations, the availability of judicial process has enlarged possibilities for competition of diverse interests in the face of concentrated official power.

The creation of the federal system added another kind of cooperative and competitive dispersion of decisionmaking capacity. In *Federalist* No. 51 Madison had found the constitutional ideal thus rendered twice secure:

> In a single republic, all the power surrendered by the people is submitted to the administration of a single government; and the usurpations are guarded against by a division of the government into distinct and separate departments. In the compound republic of America, the power surrendered by the people is first divided between two distinct governments, and then the portion allotted to each subdivided among distinct and separate departments. Hence a double security arises to the rights of the people. The different governments will control each other at the same time that each will be controlled by itself.[66]

Madison proved to be quite a good prophet, though both in the early nineteenth century and in the twentieth opponents of expanded federal regulation gloomily predicted that the national government was swallowing up state sovereignty. In fact the place of the market under federalism showed workable balances struck between national and state authority. Over the whole span of national history the Supreme Court has contributed much to making good Madison's prophecy. Thus, the Court found warrant in the commerce clause to wield a strong judicial veto on state legislation which discriminated against or imposed undue burdens on business that reached over state lines.[67] But it also found in the commerce clause authority for Congress to promote and protect private economic activity on a scale that would realize the growth possibilities of a national economy.[68] In the long run, protection of state spheres of policymaking derived more from legislative practice than from the Court. For a limited period the Court drew on the Tenth Amendment to bar Congress from interstate commerce regulations which would substantially alter ways of doing business within the states.[69] But from the late 1930s the Court rejected this reading of the Tenth Amendment in its bearing on laws concerning the private market, and fulfilled Marshall's early reading, that the commerce power, "like all others vested in Congress, is complete in itself, may be exercised to its utmost extent, and acknowledges no limitations other than are prescribed in the Constitution."[70] That an act of Congress will predictably have local effects as well as effects on doing business over state lines does not suffice to show that it is beyond Congress's authority.[71] Though the Court did not finally bar expansive use of national legislative power, local and sectional interests are powerful in political bargaining within Congress. Members of both the House and the Senate hold their seats only by attending to political concerns and special interests within their home constituencies. State legislatures define districts for election to the House, and the Constitution guarantees each state equal representation in the Senate. Not surprisingly, voting in both chambers frequently reflects the practical weight of sectional or local interests based on the distinctive economies of particular areas.[72] Thus, through legislative and judicial action the federal structure has fostered and maintained dispersion of legal and practical centers of will brought to bear on making public policy.

In addition to law fixing the internal arrangements of government, various and weighty policies have favored dispersion among external sources of influence on government. These include doctrines affecting the church, the press, private secular associations, and the market.

First Amendment values require substantial separation of church and state.[73] In its roots this policy aimed to protect each institution in its proper sphere from wrongful encroachment by the other.[74] The Supreme Court undertook—not without considerable difficulty—to enforce the principle in both aspects.[75] True, from time to time religious affiliations, particularly as aligned with differences in ethnic origins, have figured in the country's politics. But religiously oriented lobbies have held to relatively narrow ranges of public issues. The idea of church-state separation has been more important in negative than in positive aspects as it has borne on the constitutional ideal. Its observance has helped limit the coercion of ideological groups on government and also has reduced the ability of public officers to cloak themselves in sanctity against public scrutiny and criticism.[76]

The First Amendment, and its values carried into the Fourteenth Amendment by Supreme Court decisions, stands for freedom of speech and of the press and "the right of the people peaceably to assemble, and to petition the Government for a redress of grievances."[77] In political practice and in Court-declared doctrine these propositions have broadened over the years—with special vigor in the twentieth century—into encouragement of published criticism of public policy and proliferation of organized interest groups promoting or resisting law's intervention in affairs.[78] The principal limitations on these developments have arisen not out of legal but out of market processes. Ownership of mass media has become more concentrated and access to these channels therefore has become more subject to tight circles of control. Lobbies have become more bureaucratized and have learned to use grassroots appeals to large constituencies, increasing the amounts of money which private groups must muster to make themselves felt.[79] Despite these practical qualifications, legal protections of press and private association have helped multiply diverse and often opposing external challenges to official monopolies of power. The results have shown much of the uncertainty, confusion, and rough-and-tumble that attend trading in private markets. But the country's political tradition has ridden with these features as acceptable costs of competition which it relies on to legitimate legal as well as market power.[80]

Not the least source of external curbs on official power has been the private market. The elements of public policy which have entered into shaping the qualified legal autonomy of the market must be reckoned with in this light.[81] Focused interests of those active in the market have furnished much of the impetus for demands made on law, whether for or against positive legal action. Moreover, market-derived income and wealth have financed much of the private pressures brought to bear on official agencies. The market has claimed social legitimacy by virtue of the presence of competition within its own processes. But its independent vitality also has contributed to the social and political legitimacy of the legal order. As judge, Louis D. Brandeis would leave to legislatures broad scope for making reasonable determinations when legislation regulating the private market would serve public interest.[82] But, as citizen, Brandeis urged the wisdom of restraint in invoking the force of law and the desirability of maintaining the freedom of genuinely competitive markets. "Do not believe," he cautioned, "that you can find a universal remedy for evil conditions or immoral practices in effecting a fundamental change in society (as by state socialism). And do not pin too much faith in legislation. Remedial institutions are apt to fall under the control of the enemy and to become instruments of oppression. Seek for betterment within the broad lines of existing institutions. Do so by attacking evil *in situ;* and proceed from the individual to the general."[83] "There are certain liberties which we have found by experience it is wise to curtail. But wherever you do not have to curtail liberty, wherever the exercise of full liberty by a businessman is consonant with the public welfare, public policy demands that we should allow him that liberty, because freedom is the fundamental basis of our Government and of our prosperity.[84] "No system of regulation can be safely substituted for the operation of individual liberty as expressed in competition. It would be like attempting to substitute a regulated monarchy for our republic."[85] There was a continuity that ran from Crevecouer's praise of the human importance of mingled freedoms of the ballot and the market in the late eighteenth century to the negotiated compromises between legal intervention and market autonomy embodied in the Employment Act of 1946. Brandeis, as citizen, spoke for the main currents of politically effective opinion as he sought to place both law and market within a comprehensive constitutional ordering of power.[86]

MAKING PUBLIC POLICY BY BARGAIN:
THE CENTRAL POSITION OF THE LEGISLATURE

A diversity of sources of influence playing on law and competition among these sources have been features which fostered the making of public policy by negotiation. In fact, in this country's setting and experience, bargaining became a prime characteristic of legal processes. Moreover, political inheritance, institutional equipment, and social structure combined to make the legislative branch the central arena of policy negotiation.

The English Parliamentary Revolution of the seventeenth century gave the colonies an inheritance which, as they interpreted it, put principal authority in an elected, representative assembly, however imperfect the elections or the representation.[87] On this side of the Atlantic in the gathering troubles with England the colonies found the most dependable legal expression for their interests in the popularly elected lower houses of their legislatures, and not in executive or judicial officers who held place at the Crown's pleasure. As the new states framed their constitutions, they transferred to the legislative branch the whole authority once held by Parliament and the Crown together. Thus, the executive in the states did not acquire the authority that the Crown had held to make substantive policy.[88] Influential framers wanted the new national government under the Federal Constitution to have a much stronger executive than existed in the states, but they were sensitive to popular distrust of executive prerogative. Hence, they defined the presidency in guarded terms, though in terms broad enough to leave the door open to future development by practice, and vested Congress with the whole legislative power of the United States. The concerns which the Philadelphia Convention had for the powers of Congress bore less on allocation of functions within the national government than on relations between national and state legislative authority.[89] From the outset the structure of legislatures, as compared with that of the executive, administrative, or judicial arms, has been specially adapted to making the legislative branch an arena for negotiation among diverse and often competing interests. Legislative chambers stand on electoral bases at once encompassing the whole sovereignty and also marking out differentiated localities. Elected from single-member, local districts, the lower house of a bicameral legislature is sensitive to interests within relatively limited communities. The full range of interests within the total sovereignty is usually not active or equally weighty in a given district. Thus, the district's elected representative has political leeway to bargain with colleagues in the general flow of the chamber's business on matters of less immediate concern to his constituency. Wider constituencies and longer terms of office typically give members of the second chamber even more scope for striking bargains with colleagues. Moreover, the distinctions between the two chambers in size of constituency and length of term tend to foster different alignments of outside interest pressures as these come to bear on one house or the other. For both chambers, limited tenure, related to limited constituencies, keeps legislators sensitive to the distribution and intensity of interests among voters and particularly among organized groups concerned to promote or oppose resort to law.[90]

In contrast, from the time when the national and state governments began substantial expansion of their activities in the

1870s on, executive and administrative officers have typically been appointed and not elected, and operate only within specialized areas of policy marked out by statute. They are not immune to outside pressures, but the structure of their situations means that the interplay of official and private actors is much more confined in executive and administrative than in legislative areas of action.[91] In the national government and in a minority of the states judges are appointed, and thus insulated from electoral influences. Most states elect their trial and appellate judges. But there normally the business of courts is too far removed from general public attention—by the sharply focused or technical character of the work—to bring pressures of particular, substantive interests to bear on judicial elections. Judicial jobs are high prizes of partisan politics, to some extent even where elections are nonpartisan. Yet, compared with the array of interests that usually come into play in legislative forums, partisan competition for the bench is likely to make itself felt simply within the confines of party advantage; the electoral base does not appear to exert material effect on disposition of court business otherwise.[92]

The representative character of legislatures is not the only feature which has made them prime agencies for creating public policy by negotiation. Congress and state legislatures hold an armory of legal powers unique to them among legal agencies. These powers carry unrivalled capacity for varied, flexible response to diversity and competition among interests in the community and for exerting leverage on affairs, especially in the economy.

Legislative authority derived originally from constitutional grants, but in time it derived more importantly from legislative practice and acceptance of that practice by the courts. State constitutions simply conferred "the legislative power" of the state on these representative bodies, without further positive definition, thus drawing on the historic endowment of Parliament and inviting development of authority by accretion of legislative precedent. Though the Federal Constitution enumerated the powers of Congress, it did so in the most important respects in terms of standards rather than rules. Congressional practice, eventually implemented by Supreme Court decisions, developed the working content of these standards—especially as bearing on the economy—to a breadth comparable to that achieved under the omnibus vesting clauses of state constitutions.[93]

National and state legislative powers cluster under four principal heads. All four took root within the first fifty years of the nation's independence, but their full demonstration waited on the years from about 1880 to 1940. (1) The legislative branch holds the broadest authority of any agency short of the constitution-makers to define standards and rules of official and private conduct. By the early twentieth century the chapter headings and subject-matter indexes of federal and state statute books attested how far legislation had preempted from older, judge-made (common) law the governance of market transactions (in sales of land and personal property, in regulation of corporate organization and conduct of public utilities, in management-labor relations, in consumer protection) as well as of such nonmarket fields of policy concern as protection of public health and conservation of natural resources.[94] (2) Its powers to tax, borrow, and spend provide the legislative branch a role in allocating economic resources in substantial competition with the allocations functions of the private market. Practice developed this public allocations authority in breadth and depth. Public spending made itself felt with mingled effects in public and private spheres of life, through providing public services, through government contracting, through government provision of high-risk capital in advancing scientific knowledge and technological innovations. The taxing power proved potent not simply to finance government operations but also as an instrument of economic planning. Especially in the twentieth century tax laws have pervaded entrepreneurial decisionmaking and operated as forms of economic regulation by defining taxable income, setting terms of depreciation allowances, or providing investment tax credits.[95] (3) Legislatures hold plenary power to create new forms of organization for public or private collective action. They can create and finance executive and administrative agencies to pursue ends or programs outlined by statute. They may create public-function corporations, such as the Tennessee Valley Authority. They may set terms for chartering private corporations for business or for nonprofit enterprises. They may command or influence creation of procedures to govern relations among public and private institutions, groups, and individuals, as Congress did when it required filing of environmental impact statements by those subject to the National Environmental Protection Act.[96] (4) Legislatures have authority to investigate matters of fact and of fact-involved values which they judge to be of public concern and relevant to possible legislation. In some respects the power of investigation is potentially the broadest, most significant legislative power. The investigatory power has come to bear on all other legal agencies and on the general community over a wide range of social concerns. It offers means for building and informing public opinion. It provides the chief practical procedure for legislative review of executive and administrative activity, especially when appropriations committees examine budgets. Over most of the years legislators have made only uneven and narrowly focused use of the power. Even so, within the limits of legislative practice its use has substantially affected varied circles of public and private interests.[97]

This unique array of powers has all the more significance because of the general range of jurisdiction of the legislative branch over parties and subject matter. "The legislative power" conferred by state constitutions and the broad standards of authority empowering Congress meant that state and national legislative jurisdiction opened the doors of the legislative branch more widely to petitioners—and their opponents—than was the case with any other type of legal agency short of processes of constitutional amendment.[98] This distinctive sweep of legislative jurisdiction stands in sharp contrast to traditional and legal limits on approaching other agencies. However weighty in their particular areas, executive or administrative lawmaking depend on statutory delegations which specialize the parties and the subject matter with which executive or administrative officers may deal; one may seek legal response from an executive or administrative agency only through the channels marked out by governing statutes.[99] Doctrines of standing, justiciability, and precedent hedge in lawmaking by judges; judges have made some law, but for the most part, Holmes realistically noted, they have done so "only interstitially."[100] But no formal barriers of standing limit individuals or groups in their access to a legislature. Anyone who can persuade a legislator to introduce a bill can cause subject matter of interest to him to be put into the legislative machinery.[101] Generally, the legislature is free to make its own judgments of what matters are suitable for it to consider.[102] Legislators may investigate substantially any subject they deem of possible public interest. That a proposed measure will use law for a purpose or in a way that lawmakers have never pursued before, or that it will change prior common law or statute law, raises no legal barrier to adopting it.[103] Not even constitutional limitations bar bringing any given matter into the legislative arena. Legislators may vote down a proposal because they believe it to be unconstitutional; if they pass the bill, a court may later hold the resulting statute unconstitutional. But in the first instance the legislature has the capacity to take any proposal under consideration.[104] In all legal respects, an open-door principle governs legislative jurisdiction. This is a setting which invites diverse and competing interests to come to this agency to seek their ends and bargain out accommodations.

Through the nineteenth century and into the first decade of the twentieth, legislatures made relatively limited use of their powers, and accordingly figured only on a limited scale in the interplay of diverse and competing interests in the economy. This was the span over which market processes were so much more prominent than legal processes in adjusting interests as to encourage misconstruction of the period as one dominated over all fronts of possible legal action by a laissez-faire policy. Over this time legislatures made little use of their potential for setting standards or rules of behavior, and little use of their investigatory power for other than occasional inquiries into the conduct of the executive—the classic core of Parliamentary precedent for investigation. Not until the twentieth century did Congress or state legislatures markedly expand the range and variety of statutory regulations of the econmy, or begin to use legislative investigations to examine affairs in the market or in other institutions or areas outside the operation of government agencies.[105]

Though its share in the legal order changed over time, the legislative process—and the negotiation of policy among diverse interests for which it was markedly functional—was never unimportant. From the early nineteenth century lawmakers made substantial use of two of the four great heads of legislative power —the capacity to allocate economic resources and the power to create new forms of organization.

Into the late nineteenth century the society was chronically short of fluid assets; it operated with a cash-scarce economy. In that setting the taxing and spending powers naturally did not have the prominent place they have held in the twentieth century. The Sixteenth Amendment enabled the national government to develop the tremendous potential of the income tax. From the 1930s on, despite the interruptions of depression, growth of general productivity coupled with a more flexible money supply has greatly increased the practical capacity of the nation and the states to muster assets by taxing and borrowing; the converse was to enlarge the range of policies which legislatures could promote by spending and by adjusting the tax laws. Inherent in these developments was a substantial twentieth-century increase in the variety and extent of interest group bargaining within legislative processes.[106]

This course of affairs was not without nineteenth-century precedent, however. In the second quarter of the nineteenth century, states made some direct investments in internal improvements, though often with unhappy results.[107] Congress learned that it could raise a great deal of money by the tariff; this approach carried high political risks of sectional tension, but it expanded the area of legislative bargaining and was administratively practical.[108] Congress also effected economic allocations by less direct techniques which also entailed much pull and haul and negotiation among affected interests. It adopted or fought over various measures to regulate the supply of money and credit, notably involving the first two Banks of the United States, the currency issues and the national banking laws that originated in the North's financing of war, the battles over the gold standard, and the creation in 1913 of the Federal Reserve System.[109] The disposition of public lands under terms set by legislation—emerging from a great deal of bargaining among popular, speculative, and regional interests in Congress—was in substance a major use of the legislature's power of the purse in the nineteenth century. Congress used the public domain as a substitute for cash to pay soldiers' bonuses, to subsidize transport and educational facilities, and to furnish a low-cost capital base for developing commercial agriculture. With lands granted them by Congress under statutory conditions, states were able to pursue similar policies on a more limited scale.[110]

In the nineteenth century Congress and state legislatures also made broad-scale use of their authority to create and legitimize new forms of public and private organizations. Congress created federal executive offices and bureaus for an extending range of programs which were foci of various private interests negotiating for their advantage or defending their positions. State executive branches were small through most of the nineteenth century. But state statutes by the hundreds provided agencies and procedures of local government which often became objects of lively trading within the legislative arena.[111] Though Congress made limited use of its powers to create national corporations, from the 1830s on state legislatures provided for chartering business corporations by the thousands. Negotiation by business interests proved to be the primary influence in determining the content of this statutory corporation law, from the special charters of the years from 1830 to the 1880s, and then through the creation of standard general incorporation acts in the years from 1880 into the 1930s. A fresh burst of policy bargaining affecting business corporations began in the middle 1930s, but now produced regulatory laws in such fields as labor relations, securities issues, and environmental protection, outside the frame of corporation law proper.[112]

From the 1780s through the 1880s courts played more central parts in public policymaking than they did thereafter, chiefly in fashioning a large body of common law, and to a lesser though more dramatic extent in exercising judicial review of the constitutionality of legislation. Realism calls for holding these judicial roles in more balanced perspective to the legislative process than has sometimes been accorded them. Overall, the limited role of legislation before the 1880s seems less the product of laissez-faire dogma than of the practical limitations of legislative resources. In this time society committed to market dealings the regulation of the bulk of resource allocations decisions. But through most of the nineteenth century this pattern reflected more the results of legislative inexperience and lack of equipment and an unquestioning acceptance of the administrative utility of market processes than a felt need to protect the market from the threat of legislative invasion; legal protection of market autonomy emerged more through common law than through legislative contests.[113]

Through the 1870s judge-made law provided most of the doctrine governing trade in land and in goods and services, as well

as private investment and security for private lending, law affecting distribution of loss in cases of personal injury, and definitions
of ordinary crimes and incidents of domestic relations. The exu-
berant growth of the society required law for a wide range of
concerns. But nineteenth-century legislatures lacked the resources of tradition, experience, or operating skill with which to
meet the demand. On the other hand, litigation proceeded within
familiar traditions, experience, and operating skills, through
which judges felt competent to set out standards and rules to
deal with controversies or adjustments over large areas of
human relations. Contemporaries more readily accepted judicial
lawmaking because people then commonly saw problems as calling for relatively limited one-on-one adjustments—between
buyer and seller, mortgagor and mortgagee, tortfeasor and vic-
tim, husband and wife.[114] Legislation bulked larger in the twentieth century, when a greater number and variety of interests
began to press for attention and when politically effective opinion sensed needs to bring more factors into policy calculations.
In that context, both lawmakers and private petitioners for and
against government intervention began to realize the process implications of the open-door jurisdiction of the legislative branch.
With that shift, bargaining out of policy among a greater reach
of participants came more and more to the front. The litigious
frame within which judges made common law meant typically
that courts heard only that range of information and viewpoints
which counsel for the immediate suitors pressed on them. Courts
supplemented what the parties brought to them from the judges'
own knowledge and experience; indeed, we tend to single out as
superior those on the bench who showed "accurate appreciation
of the requirements of the community" beyond the immediacies
of particular lawsuits. But neither from litigants, their counsel,
nor the bench did common-law making involve such a broad
range of interest bargaining as has come to characterize the
twentieth-century legislative process.[115]

Judicial review of the constitutionality of legislation presents its own problems of appraisal. Its dramatic character encouraged observers to exaggerate its impact on relations between law and the market. Measured against the whole sweep of legislative activity, relatively little legislation has ever passed under judicial review, let alone been ruled invalid, either in the nineteenth or the twentieth century. Courts have not been called on to deal with constitutional challenges to the bulk of everyday affairs carried on under statutes laying taxes, providing public services (health care, education, roads, social security), setting frames of conduct of business corporations, or regulating dealings in market affecting workers, consumers, or the general public.[116]

Between 1870 and the middle 1930s courts asserted broad discretion to evaluate the justification for legislation regulating private market activity. But from the mid-1930s the United States Supreme Court led the way in substantially withdrawing judicial review of legislation dealing with public or private allocation of economic resources.[117]

Even in the 1870–1930 span in which judges wielded their strongest vetoes on economic regulatory legislation, their doctrine left large scope for legislators to set policy. Four propositions allowed ample room for legislative maneuver in negotiating accommodations among different interests. Generally courts gave to economic regulatory statutes the benefit of a presumption of constitutionality, the stronger because it required that the challenger rebut all reasonable hypotheses that might uphold the questioned act.[118] At times the Court repudiated the presumption, openly or in practice.[119] But, overall, the presumption stood as the declared norm. That a statute would impose money costs or loss of prospective profit on those subject to it did not suffice to rebut the presumption of constitutionality.[120] Nor was a statute invalid simply because it operated retroactively to reduce or even destroy the value of existing investment or expectation of market profit based on the prior state of law;

legislators thus enjoyed broad capacity to reassess the public interest or to take account of new circumstances, though at the expense of old, familiar ways of business.[121] Finally, a statute which the legislature might reasonably find to serve a public interest was not invalid because it would concurrently profit a private interest. This was a proposition important to the range open to legislative judgment because, especially in the diverse, interlocked society of the twentieth-century United States, it was common that a statute would benefit both general and special interests.[122]

More significant than the courts in qualifying the role of legislatures in making policy was the rapid rise of executive and administrative rule-making. The years 1905–15 laid the foundations for the growth of such delegated legislation, but the movement took on major momentum only from the late 1930s. Nineteenth-century judges declared without qualification that legislatures lacked constitutional authority to delegate power, though they found formulas under which in fact they allowed an increasing amount of delegation. By the 1920s declared judicial doctrine accepted that legislatures might delegate rule-making power if they laid down adequate standards to guide and confine their delegates.[123] In practice legislators often set out guidelines that were vague or uncertain in bounds. Judges proved most reluctant, however, to invalidate statutes for improper delegation; in this respect they gave great weight to the presumption of constitutionality.[124] By the 1980s the bulk of detailed law in many important fields of regulation was contained, not in statutes, but in rules made by executive or administrative officers. This trend has not eliminated interest group bargaining; negotiation of policy in specialized areas now often goes on in more specialized arenas.[125]

Important as was the development of delegated legislation, we should not exaggerate its bearing on the relative role of the legislative branch. Statute law determines the existence of executive and administrative agencies, defines their jurisdiction over persons and subject matter, and provides their funds and warrant for the procedures they adopt.[126] Legislators have made less use than they might of their investigatory powers. But, especially in Congress, legislative committees dealing with authorizations of lines of public policy have established influential relations with relevant agencies. In any event, the necessity of appropriations brings recurring budget hearings through which legislative committees examine uses of delegated authority and in effect ratify or procure some alterations in what their delegates do.[127] The part played by legislative committees underlines the reality that legislation is, in important measure, a continuing process. An original delegation might be tentative and general, but may gain more legislative direction by amendments of the governing statute, or even by legislative silence in the face of administrative action or court rulings brought specifically to legislators' attention by protests or efforts at change by interests affected by what officials do.[128] Likewise, statutes in some degree set terms on which judges may revise the procedures and content of executive and administrative action.[129]

THE QUALITY OF BARGAINED PUBLIC POLICY

Experience has shown that the private market carries persistent operational characteristics which limit its capacity to mesh well with the social context. From as early as Hamilton's fiscal and monetary programs, much of increasing resort to law represented efforts to counter these market limitations. The preceding chapter noted these market defects and public policy responses. However, the country's experience included another, related dimension. Legal processes—and particularly the law's closest analogy to the market, in the bargaining out of policy that went on in legislatures—proved subject to limitations analogous to those of the market. It is beyond the scope of this essay to attempt to strike a net comparative balance between the positive capacities and the limitations of market and legal processes for adjusting affairs by negotiation. But a realistic account of law-market relations requires some identification of the law's tendencies to show operational limitations akin to those of the market.

The Focus of Interests

Left to its own logic, decisionmaking in the market is likely to take account only of narrowly defined profit-seeking goals of the contracting parties. The analogue in the legislative and administrative processes is the influence exerted by special interest groups, by constituency-focused concerns of legislators anxious for reelection, and by close and continuing contacts of administrators with groups to which they offer service or facilities, or which they regulate. Charges that special interest and political ambition have tainted lawmaking are as old as the nation.[130] Perennially they have clouded the legitimacy of law's efforts at accommodating diverse or competing interests.[131] Probably they are inseparable from operations of representative government. People properly worry about law's vulnerability to narrowly defined interests. But the overall record shows that the community has accepted the need to maintain nonmarket as well as market processes to respond to challenges posed by stubborn limitations of scarcity.[132]

Most of the time judicial doctrine and practice has put squarely on legislatures and their administrative delegates the responsibility for accommodating public interest and special or partisan interest.[133] The presumption of constitutionality is satisfied so long as a reviewing court is unable to say that reasonable lawmakers could not find the facts and reach the value judgments embodied in challenged legislation; if legislation can fairly be deemed to fulfill some public interest, it will not be upset because concurrently it may convey some private benefit. This generous formula leaves large room for lobbyists to win the particular benefits their clients want. Unless judges can see no reasonable public-interest basis for a statute, courts will not weigh legislators' motives to find whether, as between concurrent general and special advantage, it was pursuit of the special advantage that moved the lawmakers to vote a measure into the law books.[134] Judges might have used the standard of equal protection to strike down laws which reach only part of a spectrum of related problems, possibly to the gain of some specialized segment of the community, but they have applied the presumption of constitutionality with as much vigor in this as in areas of substantive due process of law.[135] Occasionally courts have interpreted statutes restrictively in settings where judges may have been reacting against the sensed presence of a special-interest lobby. But such decisions have added up to no well-defined course over the years. So far as judges may have been moved by such considerations, they seem to have been less concerned for the moral tone of legislative process than to protect the integrity of the market by curbing bald use of law by some competitors to handicap others.[136].

Over the years the legislative record has amply demonstrated the power of special interests in determining the content of stattute law. There are important factors offsetting special interests to varying degrees. Elections keep official tenure contingent, so that legislators are the more sensitive to attitudes in the general community; the presence of two chambers checks easy dominance of the whole process by any one interest; in Congress the development of committee specialization and committee staffing has better armed the parent bodies to appraise and stand off the bias of special pleaders, though in the states the record is much more uneven.[137] But legislative structure has also proved capable of affording leverage to narrowly focused groups. In their home districts legislators are vulnerable to aggressive, single-issue partisans; committees sometimes provide sheltered arenas within which particular private or bureaucratic interests can more freely maneuver; the power of committees and the need to clear two houses may curb special interests from obtaining positive benefits, but also increase their practical capacity to stall or veto positive action sought by others.[138] The chequered history of protective tariffs, of income tax law loopholes and favors, of occupational licensing laws, of laws passed to bar or impede competition of oleomargarine dealers with the dairy industry— all attest the effectiveness of narrowly focused interests.[139] Delegation of rule-making to executive or administrative agencies carried ambiguities akin to those encountered in the legislative process. By its particular focus and equipment an agency may be better armed than the parent body to cope with special pleading. But as a specialized arena of interest competition an administrative agency is more exposed to concentrated pressure than more broadly based legislative chambers. As legal interventions in the economy became more detailed over wider ranges of affairs with enlarged policy discretion granted to administrators, as budget problems became more urgent, and as an agency's sustained relations to those it regulated or serviced tended to educate it to particular concern with their wants and problems, the likelihood grew that pubic policy would narrow in focus.[140] By the late twentieth century Congress and state legislatures showed a familiar phenomenon—a de facto monopoly of power and entrenchment of particular interests in a trinity of legislative committee or subcommittee, the administrative agency responsible to the committee, and representatives of the particular affected outside interests.[141]

After we recognize the successful play of special interests in the legislative bargaining process, the overall record cautions against allowing these factors to distort perspective. A central fact stands clear in the country's legal history. Legislation and delegated legislation have produced a great body of policy promoting and protecting broadly diffused, broadly shared interests —in public health and safety, in natural resource conservation, in consumer protection, and indeed, in maintenance of the functional integrity of the private market. Matched against the relatively confined range and focus of common law and of private market transactions, statute law bears witness that interest bargaining through legislative process is capable of caring for a broader reach of interests than any major alternative, secular mode of coming to terms with limits scarcity imposes upon satisfactions.[142]

A Monetized Calculus

Accounting in terms of money has characterized and sharply limited the factors weighed and given effect through market transactions. Government is not structurally or functionally tied to a close money calculus, as is the private market. Government can go bankrupt or come close to bankruptcy, as the experience of the central government under the Articles of Confederation showed during the Revolution.[143] But its powers of taxing and of regulating the supply of money and credit give it vastly greater leeway than that enjoyed by business firms.[144] The power of the public purse enlarged official capabilities even in the cash-scarce nineteenth century; witness the uses made of disposal of the public domain.[145] In the affluent, fluid economy of the twentieth century, public spending and taxation have been instruments which have allowed attention to an increasing range of values other than those measured in money units; witness government's key role in financing advances in science and science-based technology.[146] At least of equal importance, however, has been the possession by the legislative branch of other instruments of power, including the muster of votes as a kind of nonmoney capital to influence events and the authority to investigate community affairs and compel answers, to create new forms of public and private organization for collective action, and to set standards and rules of conduct backed by official force. In the twentieth century the growth of the administrative process has added new possibilities of maneuver in employing the distinctive array of powers held by legislatures.[147]

The private market has been so pervasive a factor in shaping values and attitudes in this society that official processes could hardly escape its influence on defining public issues and aligning competing pressures. There has been the tardy development of policy conserving the physical and biological environment. The lag in part has reflected habits of defining rights and duties, productivity, and interests warranting public protection only by the presence of elements that translated into money-measured gains or costs familiarly encountered in market transactions. Timing was critical. In the relatively simpler, less dense social patterns before the 1880s, it was easier to assume that most public policy problems involved only direct, one-to-one relationships, analogous to those of buyer and seller in market. The increasing interdependence of social processes and relationships from the 1880s on gradually taught lawmakers and politically effective opinion to make more sophisticated calculations. This sophistication translated into concern for more diffuse, more indirect gains and costs in social experience, reflected in the wider reach of statute law and delegated legislation.[148]

Incremental Change

Private markets tend to work through countless, continuing, relatively limited adjustments by particular operators to their particular experience of shifting supply and demand. In the long run this course of affairs has proved likely to produce massive social changes, but changes which have gone unexamined until people have already found their lives committed in ways which they had never deliberated, let alone chosen. To some degree, since the end of the nineteenth century the growth of big business has brought more conscious planning into market operations; large firms have commanded means to create positions of calculated advantage for themselves which could not be quickly overcome by incursions of many other dealers in the fashion of an atomized Adam Smith style of market. Government, however, has the potential for far greater, deliberate management of social experience, because of the distinctive armory of formal and practical powers held by the legislative branch, especially through authority to tax and spend, to define standards and rules of behavior, and to provide new forms of organization for collective action to implement policy. However weighty the programs set and pursued by large-scale business corporations, they have been dwarfed by such government innovations as the Federal Reserve System or Social Security or the research subsidies provided by the Department of Defense, the National Science Foundation, and the National Institutes of Health.[149]

That government is capable of large-scale, calculated direction of affairs does not mean that it has regularly achieved such levels of awareness. Legislative processes have shown about as much undirected, small incremental change, backing into large consequences, as have market processes. For want of planned limitation of land sales to arable acreage and planned public provision of low-cost credit, the public lands policies which aimed at promoting commercial agriculture produced generations of farmer agitation over the terms of the money supply, the burdens of mortgage debt, and the spread of farm tenancy.[150] The country lost the Great Lakes forest as a continuing source of lumber because public lands disposition went ahead without examining the assumption that the natural destiny of pineland was to be cleared for cereal crops.[151] In the twentieth century public highway appropriations subsidized automobile production and mass use of the automobile without calculation of the costs in urban sprawl, personal injuries, and air pollution.[152] Such experiences revealed functional weaknesses of representative government that are as persistent as those of the market. Always sensitive to threats of defeat at the polls, legislators tend to stay close to voters' most immediately felt wants and fears, and to heed demands of aggressive, single-issue pressure groups. Use of taxing, spending, and regulatory powers can provide focused, visible benefits, but costs are typically diffuse, and ordinarily individuals or small groups do not feel their particular impact. In proportion as public policy has reached far and deep into general experience, relations of cause and effect in its operations have become the more difficult to identify and understand, and so are likely to be ignored in the everyday rush of affairs.[153] Especially significant in light of these realities is the fact that the most unrealized potential in the array of legislative power has been that of the power of investigation.[154] Altogether, there has been little to choose between market processes and legal processes on the score of producing great social impacts from largely undirected, small incremental change.

Inequality of Power

The private market works within patterns of unequal distribution of economic, social, and political power. Critics have charged that it contributed materially to creating inequality, or that at least it helped maintain or provided no reliable means of redressing inequality. In fact the record has been mixed, and the same is true of relations between law and the distribution of power.

Legal processes hold possibilities for reducing inequalities of position, and to a material degree they have worked to realize these. Votes are a kind of nonmarket capital often mustered and directed according to nonmarket criteria, to yield advantage to people less favored in market dealings. The development of public utility and consumer protection laws has attested that there was some reality in this resource.[155] The powers to tax and spend have armed public policy for such direct and indirect effects on the allocation, if not on the relative distribution, of wealth and income as government accomplished by ready disposition of public lands to speculators and farmers, by providing public schools for children of families of little means, by improving standards of water supply and public health and sanitation generally, and in the twentieth century, by establishing such broad transfer-payment programs as unemployment insurance and social security.[156] Special interests often succeeded in manipulating regulatory legislation to their own monetary gain, as when dairy interests procured restrictive laws to bar competition from oleomargarine. But it was a significant tribute to the redistributive potential in legislation that the power of private wealth scored its widest range of victories by blocking uses of law to benefit or protect the weak; the silence or the absence of law, more often than its positive use, worked to the advantage of those who held farmers in subjection to never-ending crop liens, to the advantage of management over unorganized labor, and to the advantage of big sellers over diffuse bodies of consumers.[157] Nonetheless, building on constitutional protection for freedom of private association the legislature's open-door jurisdiction and powers of investigation helped muster politically effective opinion to enact laws which held pursuit of private interest to at least some socially acceptable minima of performance. Thus, laws dealing with child labor, safety in the workplace, collective bargaining, and production or processing of foods and drugs reduced the impact of inequality by fixing legally defined floors and ceilings for important sectors of market activity. On the whole, judicial review imposed no lasting barriers to setting and monitoring such legal standards for the private economy.[158]

The record warrants only modest estimates of the relative influence of law on conditions of equality and inequality and their bearing on the general quality of life. Advances in science and technology, and especially in the techniques of private organization of production and distribution, probably have had more effect than law in reducing harsh impacts of inequality. From whatever mix of causes, the absolute material standard of living of the bulk of the people rose from the later years of the nineteenth century. But as of the late twentieth century it appears that there has not been much change in the relative distribution of wealth and income, for all the enactment of formally progressive income taxes and massive growth in government transfer payment programs.[159] A good deal of ambiguity hung about many legal changes as they bore on issues of inequality. Thus, the married women's property acts which spread through the states from mid-nineteenth century may have sprung more from the wish of creditors to be able to bind a wife for her husband's debts than from concern to advance the status of women.[160] Public utility regulation protected customers of monopolies, but also protected monopolists against intrusion of competition.[161] But such ambiguities do not disprove the reality that some legal regulations improved the situation of otherwise disfavored interests. To write off the law's shifts toward more equal conditions simply because public and private gains existed together seems a questionable kind of reductionist analysis; that selfish interests work in the legislative process has been noted since at least *Federalist* No. 10, and does not prove that selfish gain is the only product of laws which come out of that process.[162]

However, the country has not used legal processes to shift decisionmaking power drastically toward a state-run economy or society. Nineteenth-century farmers employed radical rhetoric, but so far as they were politically effective, they settled for using law to improve their bargaining position in market. Some voices spoke for revolution out of the turbulence of management-labor relations from the 1880s into the 1930s. But like the farmers, organized labor strove mainly for law that would foster its capacity for more effective trading in market. The deepest changes which law has undertaken in the structure of social power have dealt with factors that have worked partly within the market but have reached far beyond it—in discrimination according to race, religion, ethnic origin, and sex. Apart from the Civil War amendments, here the Supreme Court has led the way in enlarging resort to law, though after the Court broke a political stalemate with its 1954 decision against racially segregated schools, statutes protective of civil rights rapidly emerged as a major new element in legislative output. As the Supreme Court defined them, claims to be free of discrimination on such grounds as race or gender come as close as any elements in public policy to being nonnegotiable demands.[163] But otherwise, regarding the course of the country's history as a whole, on issues of equality and inequality as on other counts the main currents in public policy have been stubbornly centrist. As with the market, the norm in resort to legal processes has been to rely on bargaining out relations among diverse or competing interests. From the mid-1930s politically effective opinion has wanted and supported more massive interventions by government in the economy than in any earlier period of the country's experience. But the expanded role of government is still interwoven with a continued major role for the private market. As of 1980 there was little evidence that this pattern would change.[164]

Notes
Sources Cited
Index

Notes

INTRODUCTION: THE MARKET, THE LAW AND CHALLENGES OF SCARCITY

1 See Holmes, J., dissenting, in Lochner v. New York, 198 U.S. 45, 75 (1905).
2 Cochran and Miller (1943), 273–97; Fine (1956), 354–69; Gay and Wolman (1934), 232–52.
3 Hardy (1933), 131; Polanyi (1944), 249–56; Williams (1951), 136–51.
4 291 U.S. 502 (1934).
5 *Id.*
6 Lindblom (1977), 97, 291, 326–27.
7 Goodrich (1960), 169–204, 269–71; Hurst (1964), 16–20, 230, 471.
8 Rostow (1959), 81, 84–85, 399–400.
9 Tribe (1978), 509–10, 515.
10 Clark (1957), 58–60; Kapp (1950), 228–43, 259–62.
11 See nn. 4 and 5 and accompanying text, *supra.*
12 *Cf.* Patterson (1953), 86, 127–28, 147 (jurisprudence theories emphasizing command aspect of law).
13 See Black, J., for the Court, in Eastern Railroad Presidents Conference v. Noerr Motor Freight, Inc., 365 U.S. 127, 144 (1961). *Cf.* Chicago & North Western Ry., Co., v. United Transport Union, 402 U.S. 570, 576 (1971) (existence of agreement between private interests and legislators recognized as part of legislative history).

CHAPTER 1: LAW AND THE CONSTITUTION
OF THE MARKET

1 Crevecouer (1904), 52–56, 75–78; see Parrington (1927), 142–45.

2 U.S. Const., art. I, secs. 8, 9, 10; art. III, sec. 2; art. IV, secs. 1, 2, 3. On grants of power to Congress, see Farrand (1913), 48, 141 (bankruptcy); 5–8, 45, 140 (commerce); 45–46, 108, 153–54 (money); 179 (patents); 132, 148–49, 152, 186 (free-trade values); 149–51 (slavery); 154, 188 (contract clause). See also C. Warren (1928), 564 (bankruptcy); 397, 461, 573–84 (commerce); 479, 532–52, 775–76 (money); 557–59, 573–74, 587–88 (free trade); 574–78 (slavery); 775 (contract clause); 479, 480 (naturalization); 563–65 (full faith); 561 (privileges and immunities); and 599 (property of the United States); Wright (1938), 8–10, 12–16.

3 Wright (1938), 8–10, 12–16.

4 See Gibbons v. Ogden, 22 U.S. (9 Wheaton) 1, 209 (1824); Brown v. Maryland, 25 U.S. (12 Wheaton) 419 (1827).

5 E. Freund (1917), 192; Radin (1936), 18–19; Walker (1934), 12. See, *e.g.,* Lewis Trucking Corporation v. Commonwealth of Virginia, 207 Va. 23, 29, 147 S.E. 2d 747, 751–52 (1966); Bushnell v. Beloit, 10 Wis. 195, 225 (1860).

6 Friedman (1973), 232–38; Horwitz (1977), chap. 6; Hurst (1977), 137–41.

7 Friedman (1973), 205–15.

8 A. Hamilton (1961–79), 6:67–69, 70, 71, 106–7.

9 *Id.,* 70–71, 74, 76.

10 *Id.,* 10:266.

11 *Id.,* 246–49, 251, 252.

12 *Id.,* 254, 255, 256.

13 *Id.,* 234–35, 236, 245–49, 256–61, 293.

14 Beard (1938), 612–40; Bogart (1938), 290, 295, 305, 340, 342–46, 355–56, 370, 409.

15 Tocqueville (1945), 2:155.

16 *Id.,* 156.

17 Hurst (1964), 32–33, 42, 109, 277, 280–81.

18 See, *e.g.,* Wis. Const., art. I, sec. 14. *Cf.* Malone (1948), 251–56 (abolition of feudal tenure in Virginia); H. Smith (1950), 133–44 (prime value put on fee simple title).

19 *Cf. The People Shall Judge* (1949), 40–48 (1647 debate between Cromwell and Ireton and Leveller spokesmen on relation of prop-

erty-holding to suffrage); H. Smith (1950), chap. 12 (social values put on fee simple title).

20 10 U.S. (6 Cranch) 87 (1810).

21 *Id.*, 133.

22 *Id.*, 133–34.

23 *Id.*, 139.

24 *Journals of the Continental Congress* (J. C. Fitzpatrick, ed.), 28: 375.

25 Hurst (1964), 24–34.

26 Tocqueville (1945), 2:157.

27 For various reflections of the centrist main trend of responses to dissatisfactions with the market, see Barker (1955), 281–82, 288, 509–10 (Henry George); Dulles (1949), 23, 153–57, 199, 222, 378 (labor); Goodwyn (1976), 515–21 (Populists); Harrington (1970), 124–33 (Socialists); Hurst (1964), 562–65 (lumbermen and railroads); Lindblom (1977), 162–64 (general market focus); Lyon *et al.* (1939–40), 1:14–15, 23–29 (regulatory approach); Miller (1970), 162–71 (Grangers and railroads); Wiebe (1962), 7, 9–10, 158, 204–5, 215–17 (businessmen in Progressive era).

28 Bryce (1941), 2:592.

29 Padover (1943), 649. *Cf. The Federalist* (1907), 54.

30 Hurst (1978), 523–33; Malone (1951), 449–50.

31 See n. 11 and accompanying text, *supra*.

32 See Crevecouer (1904), 52–56, 75–78; Ekirch (1955), 12, 77–82; Hartz (1955), 180–81; Rostow (1959), 17–20; Sutton (1956), 162–68.

33 Hurst (1956), 53–63; *id.* (1978), 508–22.

34 Note the broad policy implications of the characterization of the Sherman Act by Hughes, C. J., for the Court, in Appalachian Coals, Inc., v. United States, 288 U.S. 344, 360 (1933): "As a charter of freedom, the act has a generality and adaptability comparable to that found to be desirable in constitutional provisions."

35 Locke (1946), 62, 64.

36 Hill (1961), 32–37.

37 Fuller (1954), 75–79; Larkin (1930), 57–58, 64–65, 78–81, 152–64; Patterson (1953), 522–24; Schlatter (1951), 184, 242, 248.

38 Locke (1946), 4–5 (chap. 2), 15, 17 (chap. 5), 43–44 (chap. 7), 62–64 (chap. 10). *Cf.* Taney, C.J., for the Court, in Proprietors of the Charles River Bridge v. Proprietors of the Warren Bridge, 36 U.S. (11 Peters) 420, 548 (1837) ("While the rights of private property are sacredly guarded, we must not forget that the commu-

nity also have rights and that the happiness and well-being of every citizen depends on their faithful preservation"), and Shaw, C.J., for the court, in Commonwealth v. Alger, 61 Mass. (7 Cushing) 53, 84–85 (1851) ("All property in this commonwealth . . . is derived directly or indirectly from the government, and held subject to those general regulations, which are necessary to the common good and general welfare").

39 Locke (1946), 15–16.

40 Crevecouer (1904), 52–56, 75–78. See Cohen (1933), 74–75.

41 Corbin (1950–63), 6:501, 814–15.

42 Hurst (964), 294.

43 Jessel, M. R., in Printing & Numerical Registering Co. v. Sampson (1875), L.R. 19 Eq. 462, 465. See Freund (1917), 49–57.

44 Commonwealth v. Hunt, 45 Mass. (4 Metcalf) III (1842).

45 *Id.*, 134 (obiter, legality of consumer pool to promote competing merchant). In the same year as that of *Hunt,* Farwell v. The Boston & Worcester Railroad Corporation, 45 Mass. (4 Metcalf) 49 (1842) adopted the fellow servant rule, in effect protecting railroad investment from potentially high tort liability. See Levy (1967), 166, 172–73, 178–82. Contrast the hostile attitude toward trade unions in People v. Fisher, 14 Wendell 10 (Sup. Ct. N.Y., 1835). We should not exaggerate the significance of *Hunt* for trade union activities. A generation later, judges found means to curb if not destroy union bargaining power by enjoining union activity. See Frankfurter and Greene (1930), *passim.*

40 Hurst (1970), 30–57.

47 *Cf.* Nebbia v. New York, 291 U.S. 502, 537 (1934) (no closed category of businesses affected with public interest); Frost v. Railroad Commission of California, 271 U.S. 583, 592 (1926) (legislature may not convert private carrier into common carrier).

48 Powell (1980), 5:330, 334; Prosser (1971), 208–9, 574.

49 Powell (1980), 7:709–11.

50 Hurst (1964), 15–19, 26–30.

51 *Id.,* 78–83, 108–12, 453–54.

52 Clawson and Held (1957), 5–7, 36–40, 126–27, 192–93, 253–54, 338–40.

53 Friedman (1973), 508–10; Hall (1952), 62–79, 100–109, 171–72, 299–300, 317–19; Robinson (1956), 154; Seagle (1941), 231–32; Sutherland and Gehlke (1934), 1118–19.

54 Carosso (1970), 156–64, 361–67, 371–72, 379–81; Hurst (1970), 55, 91–92, 94–98, 102, 126; Kohlmeier (1969), 251–56; Lyon *et al.* (1939–40), 2:1024–30.

55 Bernstein (1955), 90–95; Hurst (1977), 130; Kohlmeier (1969), 265–74; Mayhew (1974), 111–25, 142–45.

56 Locke (1946), 71–72.

57 *Id.*, 129–31.

58 Trustees of Dartmouth College v. Woodward, 17 U.S. (4 Wheaton) 518 (1819).

59 Henderson (1918), chap. 3; see Bank of Augusta v. Earle, 38 U.S. (13 Peters) 519 (1839).

60 Santa Clara County v. Southern Pacific R.R. Co., 118 U.S. 394, 396 (1886).

61 Hagar v. Reclamation District No. 108, 111 U.S. 701 (1884); Doe ex dem. Murray v. Hoboken Land & Improvement Co., 59 U.S. (18 Howard) 272 (1855). See Hurst (1964), 512–14; Tribe (1978), 546, n. 17.

62 *E.g.*, Walters v. City of St. Louis, 327 U.S. 231 (1954); Commonwealth v. Quaker City Cab Co., 287 Pa. 161, 134 A. 404 (1926); Oshkosh City Railway Co. v. Winnebago County, 89 Wis. 435, 61 N.W. 1107 (1895). See Groves (1939), 82; Hurst (1964), 512.

63 Friedman (1973), 498; Groves (1939), 91–96.

64 Wis. Const., art. VIII, sec. 1; Hurst and Brown (1949), 28, 35–41.

65 Tribe (1978), 992–94, 1025–28.

66 J. W. Hampton Jr. & Co. v. United States, 276 U.S. 394 (1928). See the ironic, imaginary opinion of the court presented in Hart (1936), 610, invalidating the Tariff Act of 1930 (the Smoot-Hawley, strongly protectionist act) on grounds stated in United States v. Butler, 297 U.S. 1 (1936) for upsetting processing taxes created under the Agricultural Adjustment Act of 1933.

67 Bogart (1938), 661–70, 808–10; Schattschneider (1935), 283–93; Wiebe (1962), 14–15, 20, 56–61, 90–97, 148–49, 213–16.

68 Mayhew (1974), 56, 89, 129, 155; Stern (1962), chap. 16; Surrey (1957), 1145.

69 Tribe (1978), 1000, 1067, 1122–24.

70 Gouge (1835), chap. 9; Hurst (1970), 30–46; Kuehnl (1959), 160–64.

71 Berle and Means (1933), 345–57; Hurst (1970), 68–89; Stone (1975), 228–48.

72 Friedman (1973), 400; Lyon *et al.* (1939–40), 1027–30. See John F. Jelke Co. v. Emery, 193 Wis. 311, 214 N.W. 369 (1927).

73 Friedman (1973), 397–400.

74 *E.g.*, Special Messages of Governor Rennebohm, June 30, July 16, and Aug. 1, 1949, 69th Wisconsin Legislature, Senate Journal, p.

1561, and Assembly Journal, pp. 2243, 2244; all three vetoes were sustained. See American Political Science Association (1954), 54, 167, 208, 231.

75 M. Miller (1980), 186–87.
76 Powell v. Pennsylvania, 127 U.S. 678 (1888). *Cf.* John F. Jelke Co. v. Emery, 193 Wis. 311, 213 N.W. 369 (1927) (presumption of constitutionality found rebutted as to anti-oleomargarine legislation). See Tribe (1978), 994–1000.
77 Daniel v. Family Security Life Insurance Co., 336 U.S. 220 (1949). Alexander Hamilton anticipated the Court's position, as he argued that the concurrence of private with public advantage from his fiscal policies should not be deemed a barrier to their enactment. Hurst (1978), 526–30. Where other than market values were to the fore, the Court eventually held the door open, though cautiously, to challenges to legislation based on showing of motives of racial discrimination. Village of Arlington Heights v. Metropolitan Housing Developing Corporation, 429 U.S. 252, 265–68 (1977); see Tribe (1978), 1028–32.
78 Bolling (1966), 133–44; Gross (1953), chaps. 13, 15, 17, 18; Linde and Bunn (1976), 182–230.
79 Macaulay (1963), 55.
80 Carosso (1970), chaps. 1, 2; Hibbard (1965), chaps. 2, 8, 9, 17; Stetson (1917), 2–26.
81 Hurst (1964), 128–29, 299–300.
82 See Fletcher v. Peck, 10 U.S. (6 Cranch) 87, 137 (1810).
83 *Cf. American Law of Property* (1952), 4:525–49 (recording acts); Dewing (1934), chaps. 7, 9, and Stetson (1917), 27–57 (forms of secured corporate debt); Skilton (1961), 230–40, 251–74 (warehouse receipts).
84 Skilton (1963), 405–25; Stetson (1917), 21–27.
85 See nn. 39–46 and accompanying text, *supra.*
86 Friedman (1973), 233–38, 355, 471; Gilmore (1977), 6, 82–86; Horwitz (1977), 143–44, 212–25; Trescott (1963), 97–101.
87 Skilton (1963), 398–401, 414–21; Stetson (1917), 31–32.
88 Corbin (1950–63), 3:268–71; Friedman (1973), 471, 474; Hurst (1964), 286, 290–91, 294, 309, 367, 391; Macaulay (1963), 55.
89 Hurst (1964), 293; Laurent (1959), 49–50, 64, 161, 165, 172, 275.
90 Friedman and Percival (1976), 267; Kagan *et al.* (1977), 138–44, 151; Lempert (1978), 94, 101; McIntosh (1978), *passim.*
91 Danzig and Lowy (1975), 682, 683; Dolbeare (1967), 41, 44, and *id.* (1969), 382, 400; Galanter (1974), 95; Ladinsky *et al.* (1979),

8; Lempert (1978), 112, 113; Ruhnka and Weller (1978), 190, 192, 194, 195; Wanner (1974), 428, 430, 438.

92 Hurst (1964), 334–42.

93 Finletter (1937), chap. 1; Byrne (1917), 77; Cravath (1917), 153.

94 U.S. Const., art. I, sec. 8, cl. 5; Farmers' & Mechanics' National Bank v. Dearing, 91 U.S. 29, 33, 34, 35 (1875); Knox v. Lee, 79 U.S. (12 Wallace), 457, 529, 545, 546, 549 (1871).

95 U.S. Const., art. I, sec. 10; see Briscoe v. Bank of the Commonwealth of Kentucky, 36 U.S. (11 Peters) 257 (1837), in substance overruling Craig v. Missouri, 29 U.S. (4 Peters) 410 (1830); Hurst (1973), 137–45.

96 See Briscoe v. Bank of the Commonwealth of Kentucky, 36 U.S. (11 Peters) 257, 316 (1837); Hurst (1973), 260 n. 56.

97 Hammond (1957), 723–27, 732–34; Hepburn (1967), 122, 157, 172–73; Hurst (1973), 37, 49, 57–58, 63, 78.

98 Hurst (1973), 50–56.

99 Govan (1959), 90–99, 126–28; Hurst (1973), 162–65.

100 Friedman and Schwartz (1963), chap. 2; Hurst (1973), 79, 86, 178–81, 189–92. See Veazie Bank v. Fenno, 21 U.S. (8 Wheaton) 533 (1869).

101 Friedman and Schwartz (1963), 251, 296–98, 511–12, 517–19, 634–36; Hurst (1973), 82, 83, 205, 209–11, 220–25, 242.

102 Compare the caution in Pound (1940), 367, that all major economic interests have cause to complain that law often pursues its own institutional course to their cost.

103 Friedman and Schwartz (1963), 676–78; Rostow (1959), 89, 112–26; Trescott (1963), 104, 148–67.

104 See Heller (1966), 47–51, 68–70, 84–93, 99–103, and *id.* (1976), 168–81.

105 *Cf.* Bailey (1950), 236–40 (compromises entering into Employment Act of 1946).

106 Bogart (1938), 304–9, 497–504, 533–64; A. Chandler (1977), 81–88, 207–8, 240–44, 345–48, 485–90; Keller (1977), 371–72.

107 Shonfield (1965), 30–34.

108 *Supra,* pp. 11–12.

109 *The Federalist,* No. 10 (1907), 58–59; A. Hamilton (1961–79), 10:234–35, 236, 245–49, 256–61, 293.

110 See Briscoe v. Bank of the Commonwealth of Kentucky, 36 U.S. (11 Peters) 257, 316 (1837); Hurst (1973), 260, n. 56.

111 Overt discrimination: H. P. Hood & Sons, Inc., v. DuMond, 336 U.S. 525 (1949); Welton v. Missouri, 91 U.S. 275 (1876). Nondiscriminatory regulation: South Carolina State Highway Depart-

ment v. Barnwell Brothers, 303 U.S. 177 (1938); Southern
Railway Co. v. King, 217 U.S. 524 (1910). Unique, though non-
discriminatory, regulation; Bibb v. Navajo Freight Lines, Inc., 359
U.S. 520 (1959).

112 Holmes (1921), 296; Tribe (1978), 319–27.

113 Tribe (1978), 321, 403.

114 Navigation: Gibbons v. Ogden, 22 U.S. (9 Wheaton) 1 (1824); see
Douglas v. Seacoast Products, Inc., 431 U.S. 265, 274–75 (1977).
Telegraph: Pensacola Telegraph Co. v. Western Union Telegraph
Co., 96 U.S. 1 (1877).

115 Wabash, St. Louis & Pacific Railway Co. v. Illinois, 118 U.S. 557
(1886); 24 Stat. 379 (1887) (creating Interstate Commerce Commission); Lyon et al. (1939–40), 2:761–82.

116 Bankruptcy legislation: Lyton et al. (1939–40) 1:89–106. Equity
receiverships: Cravath (1917), 153 ff.

117 See nn. 8–13 and accompanying text, supra.

118 A. Hamilton (1961–79), 10:1 (Report on the Subject of Manufactures). On later developments: Goodrich (1960), 39–40, 196–
204; Hibbard (1965), chaps. 8, 9, 17; Hurst (1964), 15–26, 30–
31, 35–40.

119 Bogart (1938), 663–67, 808–10; Keller (1977), 377–80.

120 Lekachman (1966), 112–22.

121 Bailey (1950), 236–40; Heller (1966), 2, 12, 28, 59, 60–61;
Lekachman (1966), 165–75.

122 Heller (1966), 32–37, 39–40, 69–70, 101–2.

123 Lyon et al. (1939–40), 2:733, 736–43; see Tennessee Electric
Power Co. v. Tennessee Valley Authority, 306 U.S. 118, 139–42
(1939).

124 Hurst (1970), 30–57, 69–74, 90–111.

125 Hurst (1970), 14, 19–22, 32, 74; Livermore (1939), 215–22; E.
Warren (1929), passim, but especially 11–13.

126 Hurst (1970), 74; Lyon et al. (1939–40), 1:46–48; Wall (1970),
321–22, 360, 659–60.

127 Hurst (1970), 49–55; Katz (1958), 181–83; Stetson (1917), 1.

128 Kelso and Adler (1958), chap. 12; Goldsmith (1955), 146–48.

129 Berle and Means (1933), 127, 130–31, 247, 279, 287; E. Dodd
(1941), 924–30; Hurst (1970), 106, 149.

130 E. Dodd (1941), 931–46; Hurst (1970), 108–11.

131 A. Chandler (1977), 1–3, 6–8, 11; Penrose (1959), 15–17, 24–
25.

CHAPTER 2: THE MARKET IN SOCIAL CONTEXT

1 U.S. Const., preamble; see Commager (1958), 1:15, 100, 103, 107, 138.
2 Commager (1958), 1:125, 128, 410, 2:136; Curti (1943), 361; Hurst (1973), 200, 206, 216.
3 Commonwealth v. Alger, 61 Mass. (7 Cushing) 53, 84–85 (1851); see Taney, C. J., in the License Cases, 46 U.S. (5 Howard) 504, 583 (1846).
4 Holmes, J., for the Court, in Hudson County Water Co. v. McCarter, 209 U.S. 349, 355 (1908).
5 *Cf.* R. Benedict (1946), 232, 233, and Sumner (1947), 2:718 (contrasting views of anthropologists).
6 Contracts: Diamond Match Co. v. Roeber, 106 N.Y. 473, 13 N.E. 419 (1887); Williams v. Phelps, 16 Wis. 80 (1862). Personal injury torts: Brown v. Kendall, 60 Mass. 292 (1850); Guinard v. Knapp-Stout & Co., 95 Wis. 482, 70 N.W. 671 (1897). Theft: Morisette v. United States, 324 U.S. 246 (1952).
7 Lindblom (1977), chap. 6.
8 Hurst (1960), 93–101; Lynd and Lynd (1929), 446–57; Rosenberg (1962), chap. 12; Sydenstricker (1934), 625–32.
9 Murphy (1961), 47–48, 140–47.
10 Kapp (1950), chaps. 4, 5, 6; Laitos (1980), 25–27, 225, 267, 306, 362; Lyon *et al.* (1939–40), 1:458–66.
11 See Holmes, J., dissenting, in Lochner v. New York, 198 U.S. 45, 75–76 (1905).
12 Holmes, J., for the Court, in Diamond Glue Co. v. United States Glue Co., 187 U.S. 611, 616 (1903).
13 Ciriacy-Wantrup (1952), 13, 54–55, 70; S. Hays (1959), 126, 130, 141–46; Hurst (1964), 36–40, 44, 50, 59, 85, 94, 111–12, 122, 124, 128, 135, 220–21, 262–63, 410, 468, 541, 602–3; Kapp (1950), 228–32; Murphy (1967), 211–29.
14 Hurst (1964), 410, 602–3; Murphy (1961), 47, 66–69; Stone (1972), 459–63; Tribe (1978), 85–86.
15 Hurst (1964), 112, 128.
16 L. Friedman (1973), 384–85; Landis (1938), 6–8, 15–16, 34–36; Stewart (1975), 1689–91, 1703–11, 1723–47.
17 United States v. SCRAP, 412 U.S. 669 (1973); *cf.* Sierra Club v. Morton, 405 U.S. 727 (1972) (wholly public or ideological interest in environment will not confer standing, but club members' in-

dividual interests as consumers of outdoor recreational facilities will suffice). See Stewart (1975), 1723–47.

18 Tribe (1978), 79–101.

19 *Cf.* A. Hamilton (1961–79), 10:1, 266 (distaste for risk in ordinary course of business); Kahn (1966), 19, 23 (weight of incremental choices); A. Smith (1926), 1:398, 400 (market dealers "led by an invisible hand").

20 Duffy (1978), 134, 144, 259; Hacker and Zahler (1952), 99–101, 248–52; Heer (1934), 1357–61; McKenzie (1934), 461–67; Ogburn and Gilfillan (1934), 141, 157–58; Wiley and Rice (1934), 172–80.

21 Bernstein (1955), 71–73, 113–19, 280–84, 291–97; L. Friedman (1973), 384–86, 403–4, 569, 590; Landis (1938), 6–9, 16, 23–26, 30–40.

22 See, *e.g.*, on zoning, Babcock (1966), xiv–xvi, 3–18, 115–25; and Solberg (1961), *passim;* on licensing as a control on foodstuffs, L. Friedman (1973), 403–4, and *N.Y. Times,* Dec. 31, 1980, p. B7, col. 1; on occupational licensing, L. Friedman (1973), 397–99, and Lyon *et al.* (1939–40), 2:1025–27.

23 *The Federalist,* no. 10 (1888), 54.

24 Brandeis, J., dissenting, in Louis K. Liggett Co. v. Lee, 288 U.S. 517, 568–69, 579 (1933); Crevecouer (1904), 52–56, 75–78; Hofstadter (1948), 5–6, 12–15, 30–31, 37–38, 60–61; Jefferson, in Padover (1943), 678 (Query XIX); Mann (1949), 663–70; 686–89; H. Smith (1950), 133–44; Sumner (1947), 2:721.

25 Gross (1953), 19–25; Key (1946), 201, 205–9; Tocqueville (1945), 2:106–10, 324; Truman (1951), chaps. 4, 5.

26 Buckley v. Valeo, 424 U.S. 1, 39, 48–49, 54 (1976) (invalidating various limits on campaign expenditures), and Tribe (1978), 800–811. *Cf.* Eastern Railroad Presidents Conference v. Noerr Motor Freight, Inc., 365 U.S. 127 (1961) (Sherman Act restrictively construed so as not to burden lobbying activity).

27 Adams and Gray (1955), 4–8, 20–21, 23–24; L. Brandeis (1935), 104–24, 140–42, and dissent in Louis K. Liggett Co. v. Lee, 288 U.S. 517, 541–80 (1933); Galbraith (1967), 74–82, 87–88, 92–94; Mueller (1970), 24–38.

28 On labor unions: Dulles (1949), 273–76; Fleming (1957), 125, 128, 148–52. On antitrust regulation: Letwin (1965), 95–99, 273–78; Mueller (1970), 142–59. On spending: Bator (1960), 12–36; Cochran (1957), 110, 127, 133–39, 160; Hacker and Zahler (1952), 510–11, 517–19.

29 Cohen (1933), 57, 75, 78; Coker (1938), 2:23–29, 34; Creve-couer (1904), 52–56, 75–78; A. Hamilton (1961–79), 10:252, 255, 256; W. Hamilton (1932), 2:117, 119, 124, 128 n. 38, 131; Hartz (1955), 17–20, 50–56, 74–76, 111–13; Larkin (1930), 31–33, 38–53, 68.

30 Epstein (1979), 93, 94, 96; Havighurst (1961), 115–20; Pound (1909), 482–84; Simpson (1979), 566, 568, 582, 585, 600, 601.

31 Uniform Commercial Code, Sales, sec. 2-302 (1952); Corbin (1950–63), 1:552.

32 Munn v. Illinois, 94 U.S. 113, 131–32 (1876).

33 L. Friedman (1973), 390–96; Kirkland (1965), 42–58; Lyon *et al.* (1939–40), 2;626–71, 758–82.

34 Hunt (1958), 82–87, 101–3, 126–30; Hurst (1964), 549–54, 560–65.

35 *Cf.* Tocqueville (1945), 2:289 ("the notion of secondary powers placed between the sovereign and his subjects").

36 Cary (1967), 43–44, 57–59, 67–68; L. Friedman (1973), 384–85, 389, 396, 403–5; Landis (1937), 7–12, 46; Keller (1977), 414–17.

37 E. Brandeis (1957), 196–97, 217–30; Dulles (1949), 273–76; Fleming (1957), 148–52.

38 Dulles (1949), 205–6; Seidman (1967), vii, xvii.

39 L. Friedman (1973), 489–94. On exemption of small employers, see, *e.g.,* Wis. Stats., 1979, 102.04(1) (workers' compensation).

40 *N.Y. Times,* Jan. 4, 1981, sec. 3, p. 1, col. 2.

41 A. Smith (1926–30), 1:117.

42 Hurst (1973), 170–71.

43 Letwin (1965), 42, 45–46, 50, 52, 96; Lyon *et al.* (1939–40), 1:253–56; Thorelli (1955), 17–19, 29, 38, 53, 229, 571.

44 A. Chandler (1977), 14, 79, 286, 331, 345, 485; Hurst (1956), 80–81; Mueller (1970), 24–29.

45 United States v. E. C. Knight Co., 156 U.S. 1 (1895); see Letwin (1965), 162–67.

46 Northern Securities Co. v. United States, 193 U.S. 197 (1904); Swift and Co. v. United States, 196 U.S. 375 (1905); see Letwin (1965), 200–217; Thorelli (1955), 470–77.

47 United States v. United States Steel Corporation, 251 U.S. 417 (1920).

48 Appalachian Coals, Inc., v. United States, 288 U.S. 344, 359–60 (1933).

49 Hawley (1966), chaps. 22, 23; Hurst (1977), 258–59; Mueller (1970), 156–59.

50 Standard Oil Co. v. United States, 221 U.S. 1, 58, 61, 62 75 (1911); see Blair (1972), 561–63; Mueller (1970), 91–94.

51 United States v. Socony-Vacuum Oil Co., 310 U.S. 150 (1940); United States v. Trenton Potteries Co., 273 U.S. 392 (1927); see Blair (1972), 575–81.

52 See Hearing before Subcommittees of the Select Committee on Small Business, June 29, 1967, 90th Cong., 1st Sess. (Washington, D.C.: U.S. Government Printing Office, 1967) (testimony of Professors Walter Adams and John Kenneth Galbraith, Willard F. Mueller, chief economist of the Federal Trade Commission, and Assistant Attorney General Donald F. Turner on the question "Are Planning and Regulation Replacing Competition in the New Industrial State?").

53 Duffy (1978), 38–40; Mueller (1970), 86–88, 142–43.

54 Blair (1972), 580–89; Kaysen and Turner (1965), 25–41, 110–19; Mueller (1970), 85–97.

55 United States v. Aluminum Co. of America, 148 F.2d 416 (2nd Cir. 1945); see Blair (1972), 3–7, 558–70; A. Chandler (1977), 375–76.

56 Bell (1973), 196–98; Blair (1972), 95–98, 114–51; Kaysen and Turner (1965), 83–85; Schumpeter (1947), 87, 92, 117–18.

57 A. Chandler (1977), 375–76; Galbraith (1967), 184–88.

58 Kaysen and Turner (1965), 19–22; Mueller (1970), 142–43, 146–47, 154–55, 157–59.

59 Adams and Gray (1955), 52–54, 71, 75–95, 115–16, 163; Blair (1972), chap. 15; Kaysen and Turner (1965), 215–19, 230–31.

60 Hammond (1957), 80–85, 189–91, 198, 364, 494–99, 516, 549–71, 688–704; Hurst (1973), 137–45, 152–72, 176–95; Trescott (1963), 16–40, 69–70, 89–109, 144–46, 149–57.

61 Hammond (1957), chaps. 11, 12; Hurst (1973), 158–72; W. Smith (1953), chaps. 9, 10.

62 Hammond (1957), 725–34; Hurst (1973), 176–81; Trescott (1963), 182–95.

63 L. Chandler (1958), 4–6; Friedman and Schwartz (1963), 184–96; Hurst (1973), 182–95.

64 Friedman and Schwartz (1963), 44–49, 113–19, 168–72; Goodwyn (1976), 149–53, 166–71; Hurst (1973), 176–80, 182–90.

65 Barker (1955), 330, 418, 420; Beer (1926), 70–88; Keller (1977), 280–83, 374–75, 503–6, 571–87.

66 Friedman and Schwartz (1963), 296–98, 357–59, 620–36; Hurst (1973), 83, 205, 209–11, 220–23, 226, 229, 242, 244, 255.

67 Bator (1960), 12–16, 19–25; A. Chandler (1977), 495–97; Hacker and Zahler (1952), 379–85, 394–401, 439–43, 449–52; Rostow (1959), 127–43.

68 Norman v. Baltimore & Ohio R.R., 294 U.S. 240 (1935); Ferry v. United States, 294 U.S. 330 (1935); see Hart (1935), 1057.

69 Home Building and Loan Association v. Blaisdell, 290 U.S. 398 (1934).

70 *Id.*, 422, 436, 437, 442, 444.

71 Bailey (1950), chaps. 1, 2; Duffy (1978), 27–28; Heller (1966), 1–2, 12–13, 19–21, 52–53, 58–61; Hurst (1973), 216–18.

72 Heller (1966), 32–40, 68, 70–73, 112–16; Lekachman (1966), 196–97, 238, 270, 274–84, 293–94.

73 Duffy (1978), 158–64; Stein (1969), 94–98, 190–93, 324–45, 382–84; Thurow (1980), 43–46, 55–59, 62–75.

74 Providence Bank v. Billings, 29 U.S. (4 Peters), 514, 561 (1830).

75 *Id.*, 563.

76 Proprietors of the Charles River Bridge v. Proprietors of the Warren Bridge, 36 U.S. (11 Peters), 420, 547 (1837).

77 Stone v. Mississippi, 101 U.S. 814 (1880).

78 *Id.*, 820–21. *Cf.* United States Trust Co. of New York v. New Jersey, 431 U.S. 1, 22–23 (1977) (obiter, reaffirmation of retention of police power).

79 Butchers' Union Slaughter-House & Livestock Landing Co. v. Crescent City Live-Stock Landing and Slaughter-House Co., 111 U.S. 746 (1884); Northwestern Fertilizing Co. v. Hyde Park, 97 U.S. 659 (1878); Beer Co. v. Massachusetts, 97 U.S. 25 (1878).

80 See nn. 69 and 70, and accompanying text, *supra*.

81 Gates (1963a), 316–18; Hurst (1964), 16, 18, 24–34, 37–39, 51, 66, 94, 125; Lyon *et al.* (1939–40), 2:864–67; Rohrbough (1968), 295–302.

82 Goodrich (1960), chap. 8.

83 Bogue (1955), 2–5, 268–72; Danhof (1963), 257–62; Gates (1943), 59–60, 102, and *id.* (1954), 51–52, 99, 238–41; Hurst (1964), 39, 471.

84 Keller (1977), 162–63, 195–96, 376–80; Krooss (1955), 316, 495–98; Lyon *et al.* (1939–40), 2:602–15.

85 Bator (1960), 27–28; Lyon *et al.* (1939–40), 2:747–49, 833–47, 869, 1114, 1118, 1122, 1126; Thurow (1980), 13–14; Wooddy (1934), 1325–27.

86 Baldwin (1966), 559, 573; Hurst (1977), 198–202; Price (1965), 57–59, 67–73, 125–29. See also Berle (1963), 132–35 (govern-

ment guidance of capital flows regarding public facilities, housing, rural electrification, current agricultural operations, ship subsidies, public guarantees of private loans).

87 Bogart (1938), 414, 751–55; Hurst (1956), 55–56, 60, 66, 69; Keller (1977), 445–47.

88 Curti (1943), 351–52, 360–63, 489, 518–19, 601, and *id.* (1946), 107, 186; Faulkner (1938), 365–67, 455–56; Hacker and Kendrick (1936), 242–43, 249–50, 690–92; Keller (1977), 131–36, 215–16, 234–35, 473–86.

89 Berle (1963), 127–32; Gay and Wolman (1934), 238–52; Hurst (1970), 23–26, 32, 34, 47, 56, 69–70.

90 Hurst (1964), 67, 100, 107, 113, 119, 125, 461. *Cf.* Ciriacy-Wantrup (1952), 14–15, 276, and Hays (1959), 31–48 (growth of concern for resource exhaustion).

91 L. Friedman (1973), 162–63, 400–403; Keller (1977), 123–24, 499–500; Lynd and Lynd (1929), 445–57; Roosevelt (1925), 79–81, 479–80; Rosenberg (1962), 82–98, 142–50, 184–212, 228–34.

92 A. Chandler (1977), 354–56, 474–75; Laitos (1980), 6–8, 292–96; Thurow (1980), 106, 109–10, 123–25; Turner (1970), chaps. 3, 4.

93 N.Y. Laws, 1910, chap. 674, and Wis. Laws, 1911, chap. 50 (workers' compensation); 83 Stat. 852, 42 U.S.C., sec. 4321 *et seq.* (National Environmental Policy Act of 1969). See Anderson (1973), 4–14 (NEPA); Larson (1952), 1:33–39 (workers' compensation).

94 Friedman (1973), 404; Lyon *et al.* (1939–40), 1:228, 234, 346, 350–52, 357–60; Wiebe (1962), 42, 48–50, 66, 102, 216.

95 Babcock (1966), 3–6, 115–25 (urban zoning); Solberg (1961), 265–86 (rural zoning).

96 Laitos (1980), 12–20, and chaps. 7, 8; Murphy (1961), 16–21, and *id.* (1967), 212–21.

97 *Cf.* San Antonio Independent School District v. Rodriguez, 411 U.S. 1 (1973), and Serrano v. Priest, 5 Cal. 3rd 584, 487 P.2d 1241 (1971) (differing views of limits set by equal protection standards under national and state constitutions on statutory provisions for financing public schools).

98 Racial discrimination in housing; Reitman v. Mulkey, 387 U.S. 369 (1967); Hunter v. Erickson, 393 U.S. 385 (1969); *cf.* Village of Arlington Heights v. Metropolitan Housing Development Corporation, 429 U.S. 252 (1977) (complainant must show discriminatory intent, where law not discriminatory on face). Racial dis-

crimination in job opportunities: United Steelworkers of America, AFL-CIO-CLC v. Weber, 443 U.S. 193 (1979). Discrimination against aliens in public employment: Sugarman v. Dougall, 413 U.S. 634 (1973). Discrimination by sex: Wengler v. Druggists Mutual Insurance Co., 446 U.S. 142, 100 Sup. Ct. 1540 (1980).

99 Ciriacy-Wantrup (1962), 13–16, 224–29; Cohen (1933), 9, 51–53; W. Hamilton (1938), 2:119–20, 123; Kapp (1950), chap. 17; Thurow (1980), 124–28.

CHAPTER 3: BARGAINING THROUGH LAW AND THROUGH MARKETS

1 U.S. Const., art. III, sec. 3 (treason); Hurst (1960), chap. 5; Robinson (1956), 154

2 Hurst (1978), 490, 501, 530–31, 545–46 (Hamilton's concern to set early precedent for force back of taxation).

3 On eminent domain: West River Bridge Co. v. Dix, 47 U.S. (6 Howard) 507 (1848) (no violation of contract clause in resort to eminent domain to condemn toll bridge created under prior franchise); cf. Clark v. Nash, 198 U.S. 361 (1905), and Hurst (1964), 173–74 (eminent domain power may be delegated to private grantee for a public-interest use). On enjoining stream obstruction as public nuisance: Hurst, id., 179–81, 537–40.

4 See, e.g., Cochran (1955), 341–73 (role of entrepreneurs in capital formation); Krooss (1955), 304–7 (growth of industry). Cf. Fuller (1978), 357–59, 363 (distinction between voting and contract procedures).

5 Finkelstein (1938), 2:516, 522–31; Lyon et al. (1939–40), vol. 2, chap. 21; McAllister (1938), 2:467, 492–93.

6 Corbin (1950–63), 1:12–13; 1A:339, 538; 3:593–96, 738, 742–46; 3A:467, 472.

7 Edwards (1949), chap. 5; Lyon et al. (1939–40), 1:310–43. See, e.g., Evenson v. Spaulding, 150 Fed. 517 (9th cir. 1907) (harassing salesmen, business slander, violence); Dunshee v. Standard Oil Co., 152 Iowa 618, 132 N.W. 371 (1911) (bogus competition, predatory pricing); Campbell v. Gates, 236 N.Y. 457, 141 N.E. 914 (1923) (intentional interference with contract relations).

8 On need for public collective effort: A. Smith (1926–30), 2:182, 198, 210–11. On diffuse values: Kapp (1950), 254–62. On law's monopoly of legitimate force: Hurst (1960), 274–85; see In re

Debs, 158 U.S. 564, 582, 584 (1895). Compare Boddie v. Connecticut, 401 U.S. 371 (1971) and Griffin v. Illinois, 351 U.S. 12 (1956) (in divorce proceedings or criminal appeal, where state holds monopoly of process procedural, due process forbids state to deny access for lack of money to pay fees) with United States v. Kras, 409 U.S. 434 (1973) (access to voluntary bankruptcy proceedings may be denied save on payment of fees, since debtor has other legal means of alleviating his problems). See also San Antonio Independent School District v. Rodriguez, 411 U.S. 1 (1973), in relation to Pierce v. Society of Sisters, 268 U.S. 510 (1925) (parents have constitutionally protected option to send children to private schools; state legislature enjoys broad discretion as to mode of financing public schools.)

9 On the state's monopoly of legitimate force: Hurst (1950), 290–93 and *id.* (1971), 193–200; Robinson (1956), 154.

10 On franchises as a legislative monopoly: Hurst (1970), 116–17, 119; see Dartmouth College v. Woodward, 17 U.S. (4 Wheaton), 518, 636–38 (1819). On eminent domain: Rottschaefer (1939), 692–93, 697; see note 3, *supra.*

11 Knight (1951), 49–52. *Cf.* Sumner (1947), 2:721 (1883 idealization of market-contract regime).

12 Hofstadter (1967), 189, 191–92; Hurst (1956), 10–18, 91–92; Letwin (1965), 54–70.

13 On constitutionalism in general: *The Federalist,* Nos. 51 and 78, (1907), 323–24, 485–87; Padover (1943), 649 (Jefferson, *Notes on Virginia,* Query 13); Munn v. Illinois, 94 U.S. 113, 131–32 (1876); Appalachian Coals, Inc., v. United States, 288 U.S. 344, 359–60 (1933). Applied to official action: Marbury v. Madison, 5 U.S. (1 Cranch) 137, 177–80 (1803). Applied to private action: Berle (1954), 61–115; Stone (1975), 30–34, 39–57, 228–48.

14 See Williamson v. Lee Optical of Oklahoma, Inc., 348 U.S. 483, 486,487,487–88 (1955), and United States v. Carolene Products Co., 304 U.S. 144, 152 (1938) (rationality as test under presumption of constitutionality, applied to economic regulatory legislation). For both rationality and validity-of-ends criteria in the private power sphere, note decisions distinguishing between fair, rational competition and malicious or predatory competition in determining the existence of defenses to infliction of economic detriment. See Dunshee v. Standard Oil Co., 152 Iowa 618, 132 N.W. 371 (1911); Tuttle v. Buck, 108 Minn. 145, 119 N.W. 946 (1909); Passaic Print Works v. Ely & Walker Dry-Goods Co., 105 Fed. 163 (8th cir., 1900).

15 See Skinner v. Oklahoma, 316 U.S. 535 (1942) (sterilization of "habitual criminals"); Brown v. Mississippi, 297 U.S. 278 (1936) (confession under duress); Weems v. United States 217 U.S. 349 (1910) (cruel and unusual punishment).

16 See note 8, *supra*. *Cf.* Fuller (1978), 357–59, 363 (distinction between choices by vote and by contract).

17 See notes 1, 2, 3, and 15, *supra*.

18 Hurst (1960), 17, 43, 111, 140–41, 180–82, 293–94, 328, and *id*. (1977), 46, 48, 216, 271–72.

19 Locke (1946), 16–18, 43–44, 62, 64, 67–72, 126–29; see Chapter 1, *supra,* notes 32–78 and accompanying text. See also Hurst (1960), 10, 14, 44, 180–81, 270, 277, and *id*. (1977) 228–31.

20 Hurst (1960), 68–75, 111, 140–41.

21 Pound (1959), 3:353–73.

22 Hofstadter and Wallace (1970), 27, 36, 79–82.

23 Curti (1946), 97–99; Hurst (1971), 260, 268, and *id*. (1978), 490, 501, 517, 530–31, 546. Credit belongs to Washington for restraining Hamilton's zeal for an excessive reaction to the episode. Hurst (1978), 546, n. 169.

24 Hurst (1964), 37–38, 638–39, n. 29, 452, 453, 456, 471, 602–3. See Dartmouth College v. Woodward, 17 U.S. (4 Wheaton) 518, 637, 647 (1819). *Cf.* M. Benedict (1953), 26–29, 35–43; Bruchey (1968), 142–53; Hammond (1957), chap. 21 (difficulties in provision of private credit in first half of nineteenth century).

25 State ex rel. Owen v. Donald, 160 Wis. 21, 141, 142, 151 N.W. 331, 371 (1915).

26 *Id.,* 134–35; see Wis. Const., art. VIII.

27 See Winslow, C. J., concurring, with expressed concern for the stringent limits which Marshall's opinion put on the legislature's fiscal powers, in State ex rel. Owen v. Donald, 150 Wis. 21, 148, 151 N.W. 331, 377 (1915).

28 Hurst (1970), 7, 16, 63, 134.

29 17 U.S. (4 Wheaton) 518, 637, 647 (1819).

30 Goodrich (1960), 24–44, 53–69, 134–47; Scheiber (1969), 355–64.

31 Goodrich (1960), 79–84, 110–12, 169–204, 225–29; Hurst (1964), 559–62; Keller (1977), 390–91; Scheiber (1978), 134–36. See Head v. Amoskeag Manufacturing Co., 113 U.S. 9, 21, 26 (1885) (delegation of eminent domain power is consistent with due process of law where reasonably necessary to adjust interlocked benefits and costs of using resources).

32 Hurst (1964), 261–63; Kuehnl (1959), 58, 99, 114–19.

33 Hellerstein (1963), 76–80, 194–218; Paul (1954), 685–94; D. Smith (1961), 116, 156–87.

34 Plea bargaining: L. Friedman (1979), 248, 251, 255–56; Jacob (1973), 24, 31, 66, 104, 105, 111; Krislov (1979), 577. Consent decrees: Isenburgh and Rubin (1940), 387–88; M. Handler *et al.* (1975), 163. Civil case settlements: L. Friedman and Percival (1976), 268, 270, 280, 284, 286–89. Administrative consent orders: Woll (1960), 436.

35 Bogart (1938), 283–85, 293–94, 496, 504–7, 716; Faulkner (1938), 240, 243–44, 448–50, 460; Goodwyn (1976), 10, 13–15, 26–31, 96, 115–20, 135–39, 152–53, 166–72.

36 C. Warren (1928), 552–56; Wright (1938), 7–16.

37 Usury: L. Friedman (1973), 474–76. Moratoria: Feller (1933), 1067–74, 1081–85; see Home Building & Loan Association v. Blaisdell, 290 U.S. 398, 427–28, 431–33 (1934).

38 Hurst (1973), 88, 137–38, 142, 155, 165–66, 183, 187–89, 206.

39 A. Chandler (1977), 267–69, 372–76, 484–90; Cochran (1953), 8–12, 98–103, 107–8, 139–40, 219–24; Hurst (1956), 80–82.

40 Gay and Wolman (1934), 234–36, 238–49; Hacker (1940), 252–66, and *id.* (1969), xxv–xxvi, xxxiv–xxxvi, and chaps. 7, 8, 11; Hurst (1977), 187–96; Ogburn and Gilfillan (1934), 123–24, 131–47; Wheeler (1973), 147–55, 161–75, 180–81, 210–14.

41 A. Chandler (1977), 50–51, 53, 57–59, 61, 68, 204–5, 257, 259–60, 493–94; Dulles (1949), 74–78, 255; Ellsworth (1952), 223–41; Knauth (1948), 45–57.

42 A. Chanlder (1977), 68, 259–69, 476–77; Penrose (1959), 15–18; Solo (1967), 4–14, 198–200.

43 A. Chandler (1962), 20–51; Macaulay (1966), 6–12, 31–43, 61–71.

44 Carosso (1970), 56–60, 102–5, 249–51, 496–502; Sobel (1965), 107–12, 128–31, 143–44, 156–69, 237–59.

45 Ehrenzweig (1953), 1089–90; Kessler (1943), 631–32, 640; Llewellyn (1939), 700–701; Macaulay (1979), 126–28, 131, 136, 144–48.

46 Blair (1972), 4–7, 18–19, 508–16; Mueller (1970), 85, 89–90, 106.

47 Woodhouse (1974), 72.

48 *Id.,* 71

49 *Id.,* 42, 48, 54, 72.

50 Horton (1939), 254–58.

51 Tribe (1978), 256–58, 261–65. See 42 U.S.C. sec. 1973, ff. (Voting Rights Act of 1965); South Carolina v. Katzenbach, 383 U.S. 301 (1966) (broad remedial provisions of Voting Rights Act constitutional). The Fifteenth Amendment's guarantee of a right to vote free of racial discrimination is self-executing, so far as substantive doctrine is concerned. Guinn v. United States, 238 U.S. 347 (1915).

52 Hacker and Kendrick (1936), 242, 418–19.

53 Harper v. Virginia Board of Elections, 383 U.S. 663 (1966). *Cf.* U.S. Const., amt. 24 (right to vote in federal elections may not be conditioned on payment of poll tax).

54 Campbell *et al.* (1960), chap. 5; Gross (1953), 118–21; Keller (1977), 573.

55 Mayhew (1974), 33–37.

56 Hofstadter (1970), 128–55. See Kramer v. Union Free School District, 395 U.S. 621, 626–27 (1969) (basic character of right to vote); Reynolds v. Sims, 377 U.S. 533, 568, 579 (1964) (importance of equal apportionment of legislative districts). *Cf.* Buckley v. Valeo, 424 U.S. 1, 48–49 (1976) (First Amendment values are at stake in statutory limits on campaign expenditures because that Amendment was designed "to secure the widest possible dissemination of information from diverse and antagonistic sources").

57 Dahl and Lindblom (1953), 415–18; Gross (1953), 22–29, 118–19; Mayhew (1974), 53–77; McKean (1938), 192–202, 229–30; Truman (1951), 314–19, 347–51.

51 Brandeis, J., dissenting, in Myers v. United States, 272 U.S. 52, 293 (1926).

59 See notes 87–129 and accompanying text, *infra.*

60 Breyer and Stewart (1979), 525; J. Handler (1978), 24, 25; Jaffe (1965), 521, 565–67; Linde and Bunn (1976), chap. 8; Rabin (1979), 7–14; Stewart (1975), 1671, 1778–79, 1804, 1808.

61 See Marshall, C. J., in Marbury v. Madison, 5 U.S. (1 Cranch) 137, 177 (1803) ("It is emphatically the province and duty of the judicial department to say what the law is").

62 Baum (1981), 155–59, 161–62; E. Freund (1917), 197, 199, 212–14; Hurst (1950), 27–30, 32, 73, 145, 185, 192–93, 229, 233.

63 Jaffe (1965), 521; see, *e.g.,* Katcher (1977), 443, 446, 449, 453 (what are "securities" under SEC-administered statutes; scope of civil remedies under those acts as applied to liability under SEC Rule 10B-5). *Cf.* Pacific States Box & Basket Co. v. White, 296

U.S. 176, 185 (1935) (range of issues which may be presented in court challenge of administrative rules: delegation of powers, *ultra vires,* substantive constitutionality).

64 Presumption of constitutionality: Williamson v. Lee Optical of Oklahoma, Inc., 348 U.S. 486 (1955); Powell v. Pennsylvania, 127 U.S. 678 (1888). Weight given to administrative construction: A1-State Construction Co. v. Durkin, 345 U.S. 13 (1953); United States v. Shreveport Grain & Elevator Co., 287 U.S. 77 (1932).

65 Davis (1969), 155, 158–61; Hurst (1977), 79, 153.

66 *The Federalist* (1907), 325.

67 *E.g.,* Southern Pacific Co. v. Arizona, 325 U.S. 761 (1945); Welton v. Missouri, 91 U.S. 275 (1876).

68 *E.g.,* United States v. Darby, 312 U.S. 100 (1941) (Fair Labor Standards Act); Wabash, St. Louis & Pacific Ry. Co. v. Illinois, 118 U.S. 557 (1886) (states may not regulate interstate rail rates); Pensacola Telegraph Co. v. Western Union Telegraph Co., 96 U.S. 1 (1877) (federal statute protecting interstate telegraph companies). *Cf.* United States v. Butler, 297 U.S. 1 (1936) (federal spending power).

69 See Hammer v. Dagenhart, 247 U.S. 251 (1918), overruled in United States v. Darby, 312 U.S. 100 (1941).

70 Gibbons v. Ogden, 22 U.S. (9 Wheaton) 1, 196 (1824).

71 United States v. Darby, 312 U.S. 100 (1941)' McDermott v. Wisconsin, 228 U.S. 115 (1913).

72 Auerbach (1964), 52; Choper (1974), 817–46; Wechsler (1954), 547–52.

73 U.S. Const., amt. 1 ("Congress shall make no law respecting an establishment of religion, or prohibiting the free exercise thereof"). These limitations apply to the states through the Fourteenth Amendment. Abington School District v. Schempp, 374 U.S. 203, 215 (1963). Compare Wis. Cont., art. I, secs. 18, 19, setting varied guarantees of religious freedom and separation of church and state, in some respects more stringent than the First Amendment. See State ex rel. Reynolds v. Nussbaum, 17 Wis. 2d 148, 115 N.W. 2d 761 (1962).

74 Locke (1946), 126–27, 129, 133 (protection of individual religious belief and association from state intrusion), 131, 134–35, 155–56 (church not to usurp state's legitimate monopoly of force and protection of sovereignty).

75 *E.g.,* Lemon v. Kurtzman, 403 U.S. 602 (1971) (barring appropriations to church-related schools); Engel v. Vitale, 370 U.S. 421

(1962) (barring local school board requirement of recitation of prayer prepared by state agency). See generally, Tribe (1978), 812–46.

76 Herberg (1955), 164–67, 248–58; Howe (1975), 95–118, 174; MacIver (1948), 12, 26, 48, 164; Underwood (1957), 347–48, 358–65, 373–75; Williams (1951), 315–21, 329–31.

77 U.S. Const., amt. I; see DeJonge v. Oregon, 299 U.S. 353 (1937) (assembly); Near v. Minnesota, 283 U.S. 697 (1931) (press); Fiske v. Kansas, 274 U.S. 380 (1927) (speech).

78 For early diagnoses and predictions of the bearing of private, associated activity on public policy, see *The Federalist,* no. 10 (1907), 53–54 (Madison); Calhoun (1943), 15, 16; Tocqueville (1945), 2:106–20. On the later general course of associational activity, see B. Smith (1952), 252–72; Chafee (1942), *passim;* A. Hays (1942), chap. 10; Tribe (1978), 576–79, 584–91, 608–17, 700–710.

79 Chafee (1947), 1:14–15, 24–25; 2:542–63, 579–83; Gross (1953), 233–41; Linde and Bunn (1976), 183–230; Truman (1951), 213–16, 353–68. On heightened concern about the role of money in political campaigns, see Buckley v. Valeo, 424 U.S. 1 (1976), at 16 (presence of money expenditure does not remove First Amendment protections of political speech), 15 and 22 (associational freedom protected, despite issue of role of money), 26–28 (increased importance of money in politics warrants limits on individual or group contributions), 48–49 (but law may not limit expenditures to equalize influence of individuals and groups). The Court, *id.,* 48–49, emphasized the idea of free competition in the political market as legitimizing that market.

80 Thus, the Supreme Court refused to interpret the broad language of federal antitrust legislation to warrant invoking their sanctions against use of false and deceptive tactics to persuade a governor to veto a bill which would have enhanced plaintiffs' competitive position in market. The desired application of the antitrust laws would so far threaten the right to petition as to make the Court unwilling to read the legislation so in the absence of clear Congressional direction. Holding the court apart from this interest-group combat, Justice Black explained that "[i]n doing so, we have restored what appears to be the true nature of the case—a 'no-holds-barred fight' between two industries both of which are seeking control of a profitable source of income. Inherent in such fights, which are commonplace in the halls of legislative bodies, is the possibility, and in many instances even the probability, that one group or the other

will get hurt by the arguments that are made. In this particular instance, each group appears to have utilized all the political powers
it could muster in an attempt to bring about the passage of laws that
would help it or injure the other. But the contest itself appears to
have been conducted along lines normally accepted in our political
system, except to the extent that each group has deliberately de-
ceived the public and public officials. And that deception, repre-
hensible as it is, can be of no consequence so far as the Sherman
Act is concerned." Eastern Railroad Presidents Conference v.
Noerr Motor Freight, Inc., 365 U.S. 127, 144–45 (1961).

81 See Introduction, *supra.*
82 See Brandeis, J., for the Court, in O'Gorman and Young, Inc., v.
Hartford Fire Insurance Co., 282 U.S. 251 (1931), and dissenting
in New State Ice Co. v. Liebmann, 285 U.S. 262, 311 (1932).
83 Lief (1941), 51 (letter to Robert W. Bruere, Feb. 25, 1922).
84 *id.,* 177 (statement before House Committee on Interstate and
Foreign Commerce, Jan. 9, 1915).
85 *Id.,* 179 (from *Boston American,* June 18, 1907).
86 Crevecouer (1904), 52–56, 75–78; 60 Stat. 23, 15 U.S.C. sec.
1021 *ff.;* and Bailey (1950), 223–27, 236–40 (Employment Act of
1946).
87 Hill (1961), 174–79, 257, 276–80; Sutherland (1965), 99–109.
88 Padover (1943), 648–49 (Jefferson, *Notes on Virginia,* Query 13).
See Haines (1932), 68–71; Hockett (1939), 1:116–18, 173–74;
McLaughlin (1936), 114, 116; Nelson (1975), 90–92; Sutherland
(1965), 116, 119, 125.
89 Berger (1975), 9–17; McLaughlin (1936), 190–91; Sutherland
(1965), 172; C. Warren (1928), 163–64, 314–16, 465–79, 486–
88, 567–89.
90 Choper (1974), 817–30, 840–46; Galloway (1946), 277–88;
Gross (1953), chap. 7; Mayhew (1974), 25–49.
91 Bernstein (1955), 75–102; Landis (1938), 22–30, 49–62; Mc-
Craw (1975), 175–79.
92 On the limited involvement of courts in substantive policy, see
Dolbeare (1967), 41, 44, 95, 96, 98, 99, 104, 105, 107, 113,
114, 115, 118; Jacob (1973), 49–50, 92, 121, 123, 128; Kagan *et
al.* (1977), 153.
93 See note 88, *supra,* and Hurst (1977), 83–88 (state legislatures),
112–32, 194–95 (Congress).
94 L. Friedman (1973), 590; E. Freund (1917), chaps. 1, 3; *cf.* Prosser (1971), 190–204 (statutes as source of evidence of public policy for making common law).

95 Duffy (1978), 141–42, 151, 240, 275–79; Heller (1966), 6–7, 20, 71, 74, 114; Hurst (1977), 120; Lekachman (1966), 196–97, 278–85; Lindblom (1977), 177, 272–73.

96 Anderson (1973), chap. 4; L. Friedman (1973), 166–67, 172; Hurst (1970), 119–22; Macaulay (1979), 62, 63.

97 Carosso (1970), 151–55, 174–77, 180–81, 322–51; Gross (1953), 284–94, 299–308; Hurst (1974), 11, 12–15, 22–24, and *id.* (1977), 129–32. On the limited judicial review of legislative investigative activity, see Gojack v. United States, 384 U.S. 702 (1966); Watkins v. United States, 354 U.S. 178 (1957); McGrain v. Daugherty, 273 U.S. 135 (1927).

98 Hurst (1950), 23–24, and *id.* (1977), 35–37, 83; see note 88, *supra*.

99 Cary (1967), chap. 2; *cf.* United States v. United States District Court for the Eastern District of Michigan, 407 U.S. 297 (1972), and Youngstown Sheet & Tube Co. v. Sawyer, 343 U.S. 579 (1952) (Court disinclined to accept existence of broad executive prerogative powers).

100 On standing: Jaffe (1965), 461, 502, 508, 511–12, 517, 522; Stewart (1975), 1723, 1725, 1727, 1730, 1734–38. On justiciability: Arnold (1934), 913–22, 944–47; Frankfurter and Hart (1935), 94–98. On precedent: Cardozo (1921), 149–52, 164–66. See also Holmes, J., dissenting, in Southern Pacific Co. v. Jensen, 244 U.S. 205, 221 (1917).

101 Gross (1953), 166–70; Linde and Bunn (1976), 131

102 Nebbia v. New York, 291 U.S. 502, 536 (1934).

103 On investigation: note 97, *supra*. On retroactivity in general: Chase Securities Corporation v. Donaldson, 325 U.S. 304, 311–13 (1945); Powell v. Pennsylvania, 127 U.S. 678, 683 (1888). On changing common law: Silver v. Silver, 280 U.S. 117, 122 (1929); Noble State Bank v. Haskell, 219 U.S. 104, 113 (1911).

101 61st Wisconsin Legislature, Assembly Journal, Feb. 23, 1933, p. 423 (no point of order available against "unconstitutional" bill); Goodland v. Zimmerman, 243 Wis. 459, 10 N.W. 2d 180 (1943) (no bar to publication of "unconstitutional" bill). *Cf.* Rose Manor Realty Co. v. Milwaukee, 272 Wis. 339, 75 N.W. 2d 274 (1956) (court will not enjoin legislative process).

105 On use of power to set standards and rules of conduct: L. Friedman (1973), 386–405, 419–25, 447, 456–61; Gunn (1980), 270–74, 277–78; Hartz (1948), 292–95; Heath (1954), 357–67; Hurst (1950), 51–62, 66–68, and *id.* (1977), 35–38. On use of investigatory power: Cary (1967), 41–43, 57–59, 105; Gross (1953),

chap. 15; Landis (1926), 153; Potts (1926), 691, 780; Walker (1934), 228–38.

106 Fabricant (1952), 26–27, 141–48; Heller (1966), 64–70; Kimmel (1959), 214–21, 234–57; Mosher and Poland (1964), 20–31, 35–36, 133; Stein (1969), 454–68.

107 Goodrich (1960), 24–44, 53–69, 134–47; Scheiber (1969), 353–60.

108 Bogart (1938), 388–400, 661–68. *Cf.* Schattschneider (1935), 93–94, 226–48, 250–54 (tariff in twentieth century).

109 Hurst (1973), 43–45, 63, 73, 77, 88, 170, 177–81, 187–89, 218–19, 228–29.

110 Freund (1963), 16, 28–31; Goodrich (1960), 13–14, 40, 157, 196; Henry (1963), 135–37; Hibbard (1965), chap. 13; Hurst (1964), 16–20, 34–40, 74–77, 110.

111 State agencies: W. Dodd (1928), 231–34; Fine (1956), 353–62; White (1934), 1405–8; Wooddy (1934), 1292–96. Federal agencies: Fabricant (1952), 10–30; Hurst (1977), 175–76, 180–82.

112 Hurst (1970), 22–26, 56, 70–75, 108–11, 140–41.

113 See Chapter 1, *supra*.

114 L. Friedman (1965), chap. 5; Llewellyn (1960), 5, 36–41, 63–74; Pound (1938), chap. 6.

115 L. Friedman (1973), 569–75, 590; Freund (1917), chaps. 1, 3; Gross (1953), 194–97; Hurst (1977), 35–38; Linde and Bunn (1976), 247–324, 586–635, 708–20; Thurow (1980), 124–25; Wooddy (1934), 1274–1330.

116 Haines (1932), 541; Hurst (1950), 185; Tribe (1978), 234, n. 8; Warren (1913), 294.

117 Compare Lochner v. New York, 198 U.S. 45 (1905), with United States v. Carolene Products Co., 304 U.S. 144 (1938); see Tribe (1978), 434–55.

118 *E.g.,* Lindsley v. Natural Carbonic Gas Co., 220 U.S. 61 (1911); Powell v. Pennsylvania, 127 U.S. 678 (1888).

119 See Adkins v. Children's Hospital, 261 U.S. 525 (1923); Allgeyer v. Louisiana, 165 U.S. 578 (1897).

120 Hegeman Farms Corporation v. Baldwin, 293 U.S. 163 (1934); Nebbia v. New York, 291 U.S. 502 (1934).

121 Hadachek v. Sebastian, 239 U.S. 394 (1915); Powell v. Pennsylvania, 127 U.S. 678 (1888); Fertilizing Co. v. Hyde Park, 97 U.S. 659 (1868).

122 Daniel v. Family Security Life Insurance Co., 336 U.S. 220 (1949); Miller v. Schoene, 276 U.S. 272 (1928). *Cf.* United States v. Dar-

by, 312 U.S. 100 (1941) (concurrent impact on intrastate business does not invalidate regulation of interstate transactions).

123 J. W. Hampton Jr. & Co. v. United States, 276 U.S. 394 (1932); State ex rel. Wisconsin Inspection Bureau v. Whitman, 196 Wis. 472, 220 N.W. 929 (1928). See Tribe (1978), 284–91; Weeks (1938), 4:241–47.

124 Tribe (1978), 284–89; Weeks (1938), 4:244–46; see Rosenberry, J., in State ex rel. Wisconsin Inspection Bureau v. Whitman, 196 Wis. 472, 496, 498, 506, 220 N.W. 929, 938, 939 (1928).

125 Dodd and Schott (1979), *passim;* Lowi (1969), 101–24; Thurow (1980), 127–28.

126 Bernstein (1955), 96–102; Hurst (1977), 153; Jaffee (1965), 521; Linde and Bunn (1976), chap. 8.

127 Cary (1967), 35–56; Fenno (1966), chaps. 6, 7, 11; Hurst (1977) 33, 112, 123–24.

128 See, *e.g.,* Allen v. Grand Central Aircraft Co., 347 U.S. 535, 544 (1954) (appropriations hearings ratify administrative construction of statute); A1-State Construction Co. v. Durkin, 345 U.S. 13, 16 (1953) (interplay of statute, administrative action, legislative hearings); Karnuth v. United States, 279 U.S. 231, 243 (1929) (strength of statutory policy evidenced from growth of successive statutes).

129 Stewart (1975), 1701–2, 1748, 1759, 1780.

130 Hurst (1978), 525, 527–30 (attacks on special-interest favors seen in Hamilton's fiscal programs).

131 Compare Goodwyn (1976), 10–18, and Keller (1977), 581–87 (late-nineteenth-century battles over special interest pressures seen behind issues of money supply), with Lowi (1969), 102–24 (appraisal of twentieth-century special interests built into government structure).

132 Compare Madison in *The Federalist,* no. 10 (1907), 54 ("The regulation of these various and interfering interests forms the principal task of modern legislation, and involves the spirit of party and faction in the necessary and ordinary operations of the government"), with Nebbia v. New York, 291 U.S. 502, 532 (1934) (the issue under the due process standard affecting laws regulating a particular market enterprise is always whether "the circumstances justified the legislation as an exercise of the governmental right to control the business in the public interest").

133 See, *e.g.,* Black, J., for the Court, in Eastern Railroad Presidents Conference v. Noerr Motor Freight, Inc., 365 U.S. 127, 144–45

(1961), quoted, note 80, *supra*. Compare the caution expressed by the Court in using as evidence of legislative intention material from legislative hearings, as likely exaggerated by special-interest pleading normal in the process. See Ernst & Ernst v. Hochfelder, 425 U.S. 185, 204, n. 24 (1976).

134 Daniel v. Family Security Life Insurance Co., 336 U.S. 220, 224 (1949); Goesart v. Cleary, 335 U.S. 464, 467 (1948); Doyle v. Continental Insurance Co., 94 U.S. 535, 541 (1877); Apel v. Murphy, 70 F.R.D. 651, 654 (D.R.I. 1976); *cf.* Cohen v. Beneficial Loan Corporation, 337 U.S. 541, 552 (1949) (statute may require minimum stockholding for derivative suit, though this disadvantages small holders).

135 City of New Orleans v. Dukes, 427 U.S. 297 (1976); Williamson v. Lee Optical of Oklahoma, Inc., 348 U.S. 483 (1955); Kotch v. Board of River Port Pilot Commissioners, 330 U.S. 552 (1947). But *cf.* Smith v. Cahoon, 283 U.S. 553 (1931) (statutory exception for particular economic interest may so grossly depart from rationale of general regulation as to violate equal protection standard).

136 See Taney, C. J., in Ohio Life Insurance & Trust Co. v. Debolt, 57 U.S. (16 Howard) 416, 435–36 (1853); Hawkeye Lumber Co. v. Day, 203 Iowa 172, 174, 210 N.W. 430, 431 (1926); Lane v. State, 120 Neb. 302, 306, 232 N.W. 96, 98 (1930); Dairy Queen of Wisconsin, Inc., v. McDowell, 260 Wis. 471, 478b–478c, 52 N.W. 2d 791, 792 (1952).

137 On suffrage: Dahl (1971), 22–26; Milbrath (1965), 143–47, 150–54. On bicameralism: American Political Science Association (1954), 17, 35–40, 47–50, 59; Walker (1934), 160–67. On committees: American Political Science Association (1954), 68–70, 95–98, 102–4, 174–82; Fenno (1966), 76–78, 561–63; Hyneman (1950), 50, 121, 123–26, 165–67, 339; Walker (1934), 198–208.

138 On vulnerability in elections: Mayhew (1974), 33–49. On committees: Burns (1949), 19–23; Galloway (1946), 247; Gross (1953), 270–76, 278–80; Schattschneider (1935), *passim*. On delay and bicameralism: Chamberlain (1936), 64–65, 174, 178, 183–84, 191–94, 202, 204–11; Gross (1953), chaps. 2, 3.

139 On tariffs: Schattschneider (1935), 283–88. On income tax: Surrey (1957), 1156–58, 1164–81. On occupational licensing: L. Friedman (1973), 397–400.

140 Bernstein (1955), 76, 79–81, 87–90, 92–95, 154–63, 184–87, 254, 261–71; Landis (1938), 50–52, 54–55, 59–61, 68–70, 75, 78; Lowi (1969), 153–56; McCraw (1975), 162–71; Truman (1951), 395–98, 417–21, 454–57.
141 Dodd and Schott (1979), *passim.*
142 Frankfurter (1930), 9–31; E. Freund (1917), chaps. 1, 3; L. Friedman (1973), 590; Hurst (1977), 35–38, 63–67, 129–32, 179–81, 185, 209, 213.
143 Hacker (1940), 182–83; Rossiter (1964), 36–40; Wood (1972), 361, 464, 467, 471.
144 Bator (1960), 18–36; Heller (1966), 32–37, 59–62, 74–76; Stein (1969), 88–89, 116–23, 148–51, 412–20, 428–40.
145 Bogart (1938), 257–62, 526–29; Hurst (1964), 13, 20, 36, 42, 56, 471–72, 603.
146 Baldwin (1966), 559, 564, 569, 585; Nelson *et al.* (1967), 152, 155; Price (1954), 34, 35, 36, 39–40.
147 See notes 94–97, 111, and accompanying text, *supra.*
148 Ciriacy-Wantrup (1952), 54–55, 70, 252–59; Kapp (1950), 228–31; Stone (1972), 459–63, 474–79.
149 Federal Reserve System: Bogen (1960), 346, 347; Friedman and Schwartz (1963), 628, Treiber (1965), 262, 263. Social Security: Derthick (1979), 288–92, 426–28. Research: Hurst (1977), 173–78. But *cf.* Galbraith (1967), 16–17, 23–26, 31–34 (enlarged role of planning in private market an inevitable corollary of large-scale private organization).
150 Bogart (1938), 507, 716; Goodwyn (1976), 26–31, 113–20; Keller (1977), 384–88.
151 Hurst (1964), 66, 94, 125, 595.
152 See Chapter 2, note 20 and accompanying text.
153 Bator (1960), 102–12; Burkhead (1956), 35–38, 42, 49–50; Hurst (1960), 62–75; Mayhew (1974), 87–94, 110–40; Thurow (1980), 132–36, 140, 145.
154 Hurst (1977), 122–32.
155 Cary (1967), 61–66, 67–68; Hofstadter (1967), 231–35; Lyon *et al.* (1939–40), 1:320–43 and 2:743–45, 1023–27; McCraw (1975), 165, 170, 179–83; Milbrath (1965), 94–95, 102–6, 138–41; Wiebe (1962), 48–50. For skepticism toward expanded public regulation as a cloak for private advantage, see Kolko (1963), 58–60, 283–85, and *id.* (1965), 3–6, 35–41, 45, 57–63, 233. On votes as political capital, compare White v. Regester, 412 U.S.

755, 765–70 (1973) (apportionment formula unconstitutional if it destroys or minimizes voting power of identifiable groups, though it complies with form of the one-person-one-vote standard).

156 Bator (1960), 12–16, 83–85 (transfer payments); Derthick (1979), 213–27, 381 (social security); Duffy (1978), chap. 2 (social welfare); Edelman (1964), 153–57 (growth of demand for government services or support); Gates (1963*a, b*), 315, 349 (public lands dispositions); Hacker and Zahler (1952), 42, 53, 56, 58, 361–62, 627–28 (health, sanitation, education); Judd (1934), 328–29 (education); Moore (1934), 1086–92, 1107 (health); Wooddy (1934), 1289–92, 1295–1307 (federal and state general public services functions).

157 Burns (1949), 19–23; Frankfurter and Greene (1930), 138, 149–50, 154–64, 197–98; Gross (1953), 23–27, 270–76; Hurst (1977), 79, 93, 101; Keller (1977), 414, 540, 542–46, 556–64; McKean (1938), 203–7, 237–38; Truman (1951), 325–32, 353–62.

158 See United States v. Darby, 312 U.S. 100 (1941), overruling Hammer v. Dagenhart, 247 U.S. 251 (1918) (conditions of labor); United States v. Carolene Products Co., 304 U.S. 144 (1938) (quality of food); National Labor Relations Board v. Jones & Laughlin Steel Corporation, 301 U.S. 1 (1937) (collective bargaining); United States v. Shreveport Grain & Elevator Co., 287 U.S. 77 (1932) (accurate labels). See, generally, Hegeman Farms Corporation v. Baldwin, 293 U.S. 163 (1934), and Miller v. Schoene, 276 U.S. 272 (1928) (legislative authority to set floors and ceilings on market activity).

159 Krooss (1955), 23–28; Lindblom (1977), 268–73; Thurow (1980), 156–62.

160 L. Friedman (1973), 185–86, 434; Thurman (1966), *passim*.

161 Kolko (1965), 4–6, 35–41, 45, 58–63; McCraw (1975), 164–71, 177–83; Thurow (1980), 132–36.

162 *Cf.* Hurst (1978), 526–33 (Hamiltonian principle of accepting concurrence of public and private gain from uses of law).

163 *E.g.,* Wengler v. Druggists Mutual Insurance Co., 446 U.S. 142 (1980) (gender); McLaughlin v. Florida, 379 U.S. 184 (1964) (race); Skinner v. Oklahoma, 316 U.S. 535 (1942) (procreation).

164 Dahl (1971), 71, 105, 145, 148–49, 173–74; Harrington (1970), 110–11, 114–19, 131–33, 251–69; Hofstadter (1955), 262, 281–87, 303–14; Perlman (1949), 182–200, 272–79.

Sources Cited

[Official documents are cited in full in the notes.]

Adams, Walter, and Horace M. Gray. 1955. *Monopoly in America.* New York: Macmillan Co.

American Law of Property. 1952. 7 vols. Boston: Little, Brown & Co.

American Political Science Association. 1954. *Report of the Committee on American Legislatures: American State Legislatures.* New York: Thomas Y. Crowell Co.

Anderson, Frederick R. 1973. *NEPA in the Courts: A Legal Analysis of the National Environment Policy Act.* Baltimore: Johns Hopkins University Press.

Arnold, Thurman. 1934. "Trial by Combat and the New Deal." 47 *Harvard Law Review* 913.

Auerbach, Carl A. 1964. "The Reapportionment Cases: One Person, One Vote—One Vote, One Value," 1964 *Supreme Court Review* 1.

Babcock, Richard F. 1966. *The Zoning Game.* Madison: University of Wisconsin Press.

Bailey, Stephen Kemp. 1950. *Congress Makes a Law.* New York: Vintage Books.

Baldwin, Gordon Brewster. 1966. "Law in Support of Science: Legal Control of Basic Research Resources." 54 *Georgetown Law Journal* 559.

Barker, Charles Albro. 1955. *Henry George.* New York: Oxford University Press.

Bator, Francis M. 1960. *The Question of Government Spending.* New York: Harper & Brothers.

Baum, Lawrence. 1981. *The Supreme Court.* Washington, D.C.: Congressional Quarterly Press.

Beard, Miriam. 1938. *A History of the Business Man.* New York: Macmillan Co.

Beer, Thomas. 1926. *The Mauve Decade.* Garden City, N.Y.: Garden City Publishing Co.

Bell, Daniel. 1973. *The Coming of Post-Industrial Society.* New York: Basic Books.

Benedict, Murray R. 1953. *Farm Policies of the United States, 1790–1950.* New York: Twentieth Century Fund.

Benedict, Ruth. 1946. *Patterns of Culture.* New York: Pelican Books.

Berger, Raoul. 1975. *Congress v. The Supreme Court.* New York: Bantam Books.

Berle, Adolf A., Jr. 1954. *The Twentieth-Century Capitalist Revolution.* New York: Harcourt, Brace & Co.

Berle, Adolf A. 1963. *The American Economic Republic.* New York: Harcourt, Brace & World.

Berle, Adolf A., Jr., and Gardiner C. Means. 1933. *The Modern Corporation and Private Property.* New York: Macmillan Co.

Bernstein, Marver H. 1955. *Regulating Business by Independent Commission.* Princeton, N.J.: Princeton University Press.

Blair, John M. 1972. *Economic Concentration.* New York: Harcourt, Brace, Jovanovich.

Bogart, Ernest L. 1938. *Economic History of the American People.* 2d ed. New York: Longmans, Green & Co.

Bogen, Jules I. 1960. "The Federal Reserve System since 1940." In Herbert V. Prochnow, ed., *The Federal Reserve System.* New York: Harper & Brothers.

Bogue, Allan G. 1955. *Money at Interest: The Farm Mortgage on the Middle Border.* Ithaca, N.Y.: Cornell University Press.

Bolling, Richard. 1966. *House Out of Order.* New York: E. P. Dutton & Co.

Brandeis, Elizabeth. 1957. "Organized Labor and Protective Labor Legislation." In Milton Derber and Edwin Young, eds., *Labor and the New Deal.* Madison: University of Wisconsin Press.

Brandeis, Louis D. 1935. *The Curse of Bigness: Miscellaneous Papers of Louis D. Brandeis.* Ed. Osmond K. Fraenkel. New York: Viking Press.

Breyer, Stephen, and Richard Stewart. 1979. *Administrative Law and Regulatory Policy.* Boston: Little, Brown & Co.

Bruchey, Stuart. 1968. *The Roots of American Economic Growth, 1607–1861.* New York: Harper Torchbooks.

Burkhead, Jesse. 1956. *Government Budgeting.* New York: John Wiley & Sons.

Burns, James MacGregor. 1949. *Congress on Trial.* New York: Harper & Brothers.

Bryce, James. 1941. *The American Commonwealth.* New ed. 2 vols. New York: Macmillan Co.

Byrne, James. 1917. "Foreclosure of Railroad Mortgages." In Francis Lynde Stetson *et al., Some Legal Phases of Corporate Financing, Reorganization, and Regulation.* New York: Macmillan Co.

Calhoun, John C. 1943. *A Disquisition on Government* (1853). Ed. Richard Cralle. New York: Peter Smith.

Campbell, Angus; Philip E. Converse; Warren E. Mills; and Donald E. Stokes. 1960. *The American Voter.* New York: John Wiley & Sons.

Cardozo, Benjamin N. 1921. *The Nature of the Judicial Process.* New Haven: Yale University Press.

Carosso, Vincent P. 1970. *Investment Banking in America.* Cambridge, Mass.: Harvard University Press.

Cary, William L. 1967. *Politics and the Regulatory Agencies.* New York: McGraw-Hill Book Co.

Chafee, Zechariah, Jr. 1942. *Free Speech in the United States.* Cambridge, Mass.: Harvard University Press.

Chafee, Zechariah, Jr. 1947. *Government and Mass Communications.* 2 vols. Chicago: University of Chicago Press.

Chamberlain, Joseph P. 1936. *Legislative Processes, National and State.* New York: D. Appleton-Century.

Chandler, Alfred D., Jr. 1962. *Strategy and Structure: Chapters in the History of the Industrial Enterprise.* Cambridge, Mass.: MIT Press, 1962.

Chandler, Alfred D., Jr. 1977. *The Visible Hand.* Cambridge, Mass.: Belknap Press of Harvard University Press.

Chandler, Lester V. 1958. *Benjamin Strong, Central Banker.* Washington, D.C.: Brookings Institution.

Choper, Jesse. 1974. "The Supreme Court and the Political Branches: Democratic Theory and Practice." 122 *University of Pennsylvania Law Review* 810.

Ciriacy-Wantrup, S. W. 1952. *Resource Conservation: Economics and Policies.* Berkeley: University of California Press.

Clark, John Maurice. 1957. *Economic Institutions and Human Welfare.* New York: Alfred A. Knopf.

Clawson, Marion, and Burnell Held. 1957. *The Federal Lands: Their Use and Management.* Baltimore: Johns Hopkins Press.

Cochran, Thomas C. 1953. *Railroad Leaders, 1845–1890; The Business Mind in Action.* Cambridge, Mass.: Harvard University Press.

176Sources Cited

Cochran, Thomas C. 1955. "The Entrepreneur in American Capital Formation." In National Bureau Committee for Economic Research, *Capital Formation and Economic Growth*. Princeton: Princeton University Press.

Cochran, Thomas C. 1957. *The American Business System: A Historical Perspective, 1900–1955*. Cambridge, Mass.: Harvard University Press.

Cochran, Thomas C., and William Miller. 1943. *The Age of Enterprise*. New York: Macmillan Co.

Cohen, Morris R. 1933. *Law and the Social Order*. New York: Harcourt, Brace & Co.

Coker, Francis W. 1938. "American Traditions Concerning Property and Liberty." In Committee of the Association of American Law Schools, *Selected Essays on Constitutional Law*. Vol. 2 Chicago: Foundation Press.

Commager, Henry Steele, ed. 1958. *Documents of American History*. 6th ed. New York: Appleton-Century-Crofts.

Corbin, Arthur Linton. 1950–63. *Corbin on Contracts*. 8 vols. St. Paul, Minn.: West Publishing Co.

Cravath, Paul D. 1917. "Reorganization of Corporations." In Francis Lynde Stetson et al., *Some Legal Phases of Corporate Financing, Reorganization, and Regulation*. New York: Macmillan Co.

Crevecouer, J. Hector St. John de. 1904. *Letters from an American Farmer*. New York: Fox, Duffield.

Curti, Merle. 1943. *The Growth of American Thought*. New York: Harper & Brothers.

Curti, Merle. 1946. *The Roots of American Loyalty*. New York: Columbia University Press.

Dahl, Robert A. 1971. *Polyarchy: Participation and Opposition*. New Haven: Yale University Press.

Dahl, Robert A., and Charles E. Lindblom. 1953. *Politics, Economics, and Welfare*. New York: Harper & Brothers.

Danhof, Clarence H. 1963. "Farm-Making Costs and the 'Safety Valve,' 1850–1860." In Vernon Carstensen, ed., *The Public Lands: Studies in the History of the Public Domain*. Madison: University of Wisconsin Press.

Danzig, Richard, and Michael J. Lowy, 1975. "Everyday Disputes and Mediation in the United States: A Reply to Professor Felstiner." 9 *Law and Society Review* 675.

Davis, Kenneth C. 1969. *Discretionary Justice*. Baton Rouge: Louisiana University Press.

Derthick, Martha. 1979. *Policymaking for Social Security*. Washington, D.C.: Brookings Institution.

Dewing, Arthur Stone. 1934. *A Study of Corporate Securities*. New York: Ronald Press Co.

Dodd, E. Merrick, Jr. 1941. "The Modern Corporation, Private Property, and Recent Federal Legislation." 54 *Harvard Law Review* 917.

Dodd, Lawrence C., and Richard L. Schott. 1979. *Congress and the Administrative State*. New York: John Wiley & Sons.

Dodd, Walter F. 1928. *State Government*. New York: Century Co.

Dolbeare, Kenneth. 1967. *Trial Courts in Urban Politics*. New York: John Wiley & Sons.

Dolbeare, Kenneth. 1969. *The Federal District Courts and Urban Policy: An Exploratory Study*. New York: John Wiley & Sons.

Duffy, James. 1978. *Domestic Affairs*. New York: Simon & Schuster.

Dulles, Foster Rhea. 1949. *Labor in America*. New York: Thomas Y. Crowell Co.

Edelman, Murray. 1964. *The Symbolic Uses of Politics*. Urbana: University of Illinois Press.

Edwards, Corwin D. 1949. *Maintaining Competition: Requisites of a Governmental Policy*. New York: McGraw-Hill Book Co.

Ehrenzweig, Albert A. 1953. "Adhesion Contracts in the Conflict of Laws." 53 *Columbia Law Review* 1072.

Ekirch, Arthur A., Jr. 1955. *The Decline of American Liberalism*. New York: Longmans, Green & Co.

Ellsworth, John S., Jr. 1952. *Factory Folkways*. New Haven: Yale University Press.

Epstein, Richard A. 1979. "Unconscionability: A Critical Reappraisal." In A. Kronman and Richard Posner, *The Economics of Contract Law*. Boston: Little, Brown & Co.

Fabricant, Solomon. 1952. *The Trend of Government Activity in the United States since 1900*. New York: National Bureau of Economic Research.

Farrand, Max. 1913. *The Framing of the Constitution of the United States*. New Haven: Yale University Press.

Faulkner, Harold U. 1938. *American Economic History*. 4th ed. New York: Harper & Brothers.

The Federalist. 1907. Ed. Henry Cabot Lodge. New York: G. P. Putnam's Sons.

Feller, Abraham H. 1933. "Moratory Legislation: A Comparative Study." 46 *Harvard Law Review* 1061.

Fenno, Richard F., Jr. 1966. *The Power of the Purse: Appropriations Politics in Congress*. Boston: Little, Brown & Co.

Fine, Sidney. 1956. *Laissez Faire and the General-Welfare State*. Ann Arbor: University of Michigan Press.

Finkelstein, Maurice. 1938. "From Munn v. Illinois to Tyson v. Banton: A Study in the Judicial Process." *Selected Essays on Constitutional Law*. Vol. 2. Chicago: Foundation Press.

Finletter, Thomas K. 1937. *Principles of Corporate Reorganization in Bankruptcy*. Charlottesville, Va.: Michie Co.

Fleming, Robben W. 1957. "The Significance of the Wagner Act." In Milton Derber and Edwin Young, eds., *Labor and the New Deal*. Madison: University of Wisconsin Press.

Frankfurter, Felix. 1930. *The Public and Its Government*. New Haven: Yale University Press.

Frankfurter, Felix, and Nathan Greene. 1930. *The Labor Injunction*. New York: Macmillan Co.

Frankfurter, Felix, and Henry M. Hart, Jr. 1935. "The Business of the Supreme Court at October Term, 1934." 49 *Harvard Law Review* 68.

Freund, Ernst. 1917. *Standards of American Legislation*. Chicago: University of Chicago Press.

Freund, Rudolf. 1963. "Military Bounty Lands and the Origins of the Public Domain." In Vernon Carstensen, ed., *The Public Lands*. Madison: University of Wisconsin Press.

Friedman, Lawrence M. 1965. *Contract Law in America: A Social and Economic Case Study*. Madison: University of Wisconsin Press.

Friedman, Lawrence M. 1973. *A History of American Law*. New York: Simon & Schuster.

Friedman, Lawrence M. 1979. "Plea Bargaining in Historical Perspective." 13 *Law and Society Review* 247.

Friedman, Lawrence M., and Robert W. Percival. 1976. "A Tale of Two Courts: Litigation in Alameda and San Benito Counties." 10 *Law and Society Review* 267.

Friedman, Milton, and Anna Jacobson Schwartz. 1963. *A Monetary History of the United States, 1867–1960*. Princeton: Princeton University Press.

Fuller, Lon L. 1954. "Some Reflections on Legal and Economic Freedoms." 54 *Columbia Law Review* 70.

Fuller, Lon L. 1978. "The Forms and Limits of Adjudication." 92 Harvard Law Review 353.

Galanter, Marc. 1974. "Why the 'Haves' Come Out Ahead." 9 *Law and Society Review* 95.

Galbraith, John Kenneth. 1967. *The New Industrial State*. Boston: Houghton, Mifflin Co.

Galloway, George B. 1946. *Congress at the Crossroads*. New York: Thomas Y. Crowell Co.

Gates, Paul Wallace. 1943. *The Wisconsin Pine Lands of Cornell University*. Ithaca, N.Y.: Cornell University Press.

Gates, Paul Wallace. 1954. *Fifty Million Acres: Conflicts over Kansas Land Policy, 1854–1890*. Ithaca, N.Y.: Cornell University Press.

Gates, Paul Wallace. 1963a. "The Homestead Law in an Incongruous Land System." In Vernon Carstensen, ed., *The Public Lands*. Madison: University of Wisconsin Press.

Gates, Paul Wallace. 1963b. "The Role of the Land Speculator in Western Development." *Id.*

Gay, Edwin F., and Leo Wolman. 1934. "Trends in Economic Organization." In President's Research Committee on Social Trends, *Recent Social Trends in the United States*. New York: Whittlesey House, McGraw-Hill Book Co.

Gilmore, Grant. 1977. *The Ages of American Law*. New Haven: Yale University Press.

Goldsmith, Raymond W. 1955. "Financial Structure and Economic Growth in Advanced Countries." In National Bureau of Economic Research, *Capital Formation and Economic Growth*. Princeton: Princeton University Press.

Goodrich, Carter. 1960. *Government Promotion of American Canals and Railroads, 1800–1890*. New York: Columbia University Press.

Goodwyn, Lawrence. 1976. *Democratic Promise: The Populist Movement in America*. New York: Oxford University Press.

Gouge, William M. 1835. *Short History of Paper Money and Banking in the United States*. 2d ed. New York: B. & S. Collins.

Govan, Thomas P. 1959. *Nicholas Biddle*. Chicago: University of Chicago Press.

Gross, Bertram M. 1953. *The Legislative Struggle*. New York: McGraw-Hill Book Co.

Groves, Harold M. 1939. *Financing Government*. New York: Henry Holt & Co.

Gunn, L. Ray. 1980. "The New York State Legislature: A Developmental Perspective, 1777–1846." 4 *Social Science History* 267.

Hacker, Louis M. 1940. *The Triumph of American Capitalism*. New York: Simon & Schuster.

Hacker, Louis M. 1968. *The World of Andrew Carnegie, 1865–1901*. Philadelphia: J. B. Lippincott Co.

Hacker, Louis M., and Benjamin B. Kendrick. 1936. *The United States since 1865.* Rev. ed. New York: F. S. Crofts & Co.

Hacker, Louis M., and Helen S. Zahler. 1947. *The Shaping of the American Tradition.* 2 vols. New York: Columbia University Press.

Hacker, Louis M., and Helen S. Zahler. 1952. *The United States in the Twentieth Century.* New York: Appleton-Century-Crofts.

Haines, Charles Grove. 1932. *The American Doctrine of Judicial Supremacy.* Berkeley: University of California Press.

Hall, Jerome. 1952. *Theft, Law, and Society.* 2d ed. Indianapolis: Bobbs-Merrill Co.

Hamilton, Alexander. 1961–79. *Paper.* 26 vols. Ed. Harold C. Syrett and Jacob E. Cooke. New York: Columbia University Press.

Hamilton, Walton H. 1938. "Property—According to Locke." In *Selected Essays on Constitutional Law.* Vol. 2. Chicago: Foundation Press.

Hammond, Bray. 1957. *Banks and Politics in America from the Revolution to the Civil War.* Princeton: Princeton University Press.

Handler, Joel. 1978. *Social Movements and the Legal System: A Theory of Law Reform and Social Change.* New York: Academic Press.

Handler, Milton; Harlan M. Blake; Robert Pitofsky; and Harvey H. Goldschmid. 1975. *Cases and Materials on Trade Regulation.* Mineola, N.Y.: Foundation Press.

Hardy, Charles O. 1933. "Market." 10 *Encyclopedia of the Social Sciences* 131. New York: Macmillan Co.

Harrington, Michael. 1970. *Socialism.* New York: Saturday Review Press.

Hart, Henry M., Jr. 1935. "The Gold Clause in United States Bonds." 48 *Harvard Law Review* 1057.

Hart, Henry M., Jr. 1936. "Processing Taxes and Protective Tariffs." 49 *Harvard Law Review* 610.

Hartz, Louis. 1948. *Economic Policy and Democratic Thought: Pennsylvania, 1776–1860.* Cambridge, Mass.: Harvard University Press.

Hartz, Louis. 1955. *The Liberal Tradition in America.* New York: Harcourt, Brace & Co.

Havighurst, Harold. 1961. *The Nature of Private Contract.* Evanston, Ill.: Northwestern University Press.

Hawley, Ellis W. 1966. *The New Deal and the Problem of Monopoly.* Princeton: Princeton University Press.

Haynes, George H. 1938. *The Senate of the United States.* 2 vols. Boston: Houghton, Mifflin Co.

Hays, Arthur Garfield. 1942. *City Lawyer*. New York: Simon & Schuster.

Hays, Samuel P. 1959. *Conservation and the Gospel of Efficiency: The Progressive Conservation Movement, 1890–1920*. Cambridge, Mass.: Harvard University Press.

Heath, Milton S. 1954. *Constructive Liberalism: The Role of the State in Economic Development in Georgia to 1860*. Cambridge, Mass.: Harvard University Press.

Heer, Clarence. 1934. "Taxation and Public Finance." In President's Research Committee on Social Trends, *Recent Social Trends in the United States*. New York: Whittlesey House, McGraw-Hill Book Co.

Heller, Walter W. 1966. *New Dimensions of Political Economy*. Cambridge, Mass.: Harvard University Press.

Heller, Walter W. 1976. *The Economy: Old Myths and New Realities*. New York: W. W. Norton & Co.

Hellerstein, Jerome R. 1963. *Taxes, Loop Holes, and Morals*. New York: McGraw-Hill Book Co.

Henderson, Gerard C. 1918. *The Position of Foreign Corporations in American Constitutional Law*. Cambridge, Mass.: Harvard University Press.

Henry, Robert S. 1963. "The Railroad Land Grant Legend in American History Texts." In Vernon Carstensen, ed., *The Public Lands*. Madison: University of Wisconsin Press.

Hepburn, A. Barton. 1967. *A History of Currency in the United States*. New York: Augustus M. Kelley.

Herberg, Will. 1955. *Protestant, Catholic, Jew*. Garden City, N.Y.: Doubleday & Co.

Hibbard, Benjamin H. 1965. *A History of the Public Land Policies*. Madison: University of Wisconsin Press.

Hill, Christopher. 1961. *The Century of Revolution, 1603–1714*. New York: W. W. Norton & Co.

Hockett, Homer Cary. 1939. *The Constitutional History of the United States, 1776–1826*. 2 vols. New York: Macmillan Co.

Hofstadter, Richard. 1948. *The American Political Tradition and the Men Who Made It*. New York: Alfred A. Knopf.

Hofstadter, Richard. 1955. *The Age of Reform: From Bryan to F.D.R.* New York: Alfred A. Knopf.

Hofstadter, Richard. 1967. *The Paranoid Style in American Politics*. New York: Vintage Books.

Hofstadter, Richard. 1970. *The Idea of a Party System*. Berkeley: University of California Press.

Hofstadter, Richard, and Michael Wallace, eds. 1970. *American Violence: A Documentary History.* New York: Alfred A. Knopf.

Holmes, Oliver Wendell, Jr. 1881. *The Common Law.* Boston: Little, Brown & Co.

Holmes, Oliver Wendell, Jr. 1921. *Collected Legal Papers.* New York: Harcourt, Brace & Co.

Horton, John Theodore. 1939. *James Kent: A Study in Conservatism, 1763–1847.* New York: D. Appleton-Century Co.

Horwitz, Morton J. 1977. *The Transformation of American Law, 1780–1860.* Cambridge, Mass.: Harvard University Press.

Howe, Mark DeWolfe. 1965. *The Garden and the Wilderness: Religion and Government in American Constitutional History.* Chicago: Phoenix Books, University of Chicago Press.

Hunt, Robert S. 1958. *Law and Locomotives.* Madison: State Historical Society of Wisconsin.

Hurst, James Willard. 1950. *The Growth of American Law: The Law Makers.* Boston: Little, Brown & Co.

Hurst, James Willard. 1956. *Law and the Conditions of Freedom in the Nineteenth-Century United States.* Madison: University of Wisconsin Press.

Hurst, James Willard. 1960. *Law and Social Process in United States History.* Ann Arbor: University of Michigan Law School.

Hurst, James Willard. 1964. *Law and Economic Growth: The Legal History of the Lumber Industry in Wisconsin, 1836–1915.* Cambridge, Mass.: Belknap Press of Harvard University Press.

Hurst, James Willard. 1970. *The Legitimacy of the Business Corporation in the Law of the United States, 1780–1970.* Charlottesville: University Press of Virginia.

Hurst, James Willard. 1971. *The Law of Treason in the United States.* Westport, Conn.: Greenwood Press.

Hurst, James Willard. 1973. *A Legal History of Money in the United States, 1774–1970.* Lincoln: University of Nebraska Press.

Hurst, James Willard. 1974. "Watergate: Some Basic Issues." 7 *The Center Magazine* 11.

Hurst, James Willard. 1977. *Law and Social Order in the United States.* Ithaca, N.Y.: Cornell University Press.

Hurst, James Willard. 1978. "Alexander Hamilton, Law Maker." 78 *Columbia Law Review* 483.

Hurst, James Willard, and Betty R. Brown. 1949. "The Perils of the Test Case." 1949 *Wisconsin Law Review* 26.

Hyneman, Charles S. 1950. *Bureaucracy in a Democracy*. New York: Harper & Brothers.

Isenburgh, Maxwell S., and Seymour J. Rubin. 1940. "Antitrust Enforcement through Consent Decrees." 53 *Harvard Law Review*.

Jacob, Herbert. 1973. *Urban Justice: Law and Order in American Cities*. Englewood Cliffs, N.J.: Prentice-Hall.

Jaffe, Louis. 1965. *Judicial Control of Administrative Action*. Boston: Little, Brown & Co.

Judd, Charles H. 1934. "Education." In President's Research Committee on Social Trends, *Recent Social Trends in the United States*. New York: Whittlesey House, McGraw-Hill Book Co.

Kagan, Robert A.; Blair Cartwright; Lawrence M. Friedman; and Stanton Wheeler. 1977. "The Business of State Supreme Courts, 1870–1970." 30 *Stanford Law Review* 121.

Kahn, Alfred E. 1966. "The Tyranny of Small Decisions: Market Failures, Imperfections, and the Limits of Economics." *KYKLOS: International Review for Social Sciences* 19.

Kapp, K. William. 1950. *The Social Costs of Private Enterprise*. Cambridge, Mass. Harvard University Press.

Katcher, Richard D. 1977. "Securities Regulation." In New York University School of Law, *Annual Survey of American Law, 1976*. Dobbs Ferry, N.Y.: Oceana Publications.

Katz, Wilber G. 1958. "The Philosophy of Midcentury Corporation Statutes." 23 *Law and Contemporary Problems* 177.

Kaysen, Carl, and Donald F. Turner. 1965. *Antitrust Policy: An Economic and Legal Analysis*. Cambridge, Mass.: Harvard University Press.

Keller, Morton. 1977. *Affairs of State: Public Life in Late-Nineteenth-Century America*. Cambridge, Mass.: Belknap Press of Harvard University Press.

Kelso, Louis O., and Mortimer J. Adler. 1958. *The Capitalist Manifesto*. New York: Random House.

Kessler, Friedrich. 1943. "Contracts of Adhesion: Some Thoughts about Freedom of Contract." 43 *Columbia Law Review* 629.

Key, Vernon O., Jr. 1946. *Politics, Parties, and Pressure Groups*. New York: Thomas Y. Crowell Co.

Kimmel, Lewis H. 1959. *Federal Budget and Fiscal Policy, 1789–1958*. Washington, D.C.: Brookings Institution.

Kirkland, Edward Chase. 1965. *Charles Francis Adams, Jr.* Cambridge, Mass.: Harvard University Press.

Knauth, Oswald. 1948. *Managerial Enterprise*. New York: W. W. Norton & Co.

Knight, Frank H. 1951. *The Ethics of Competition*. New York: Augustus M. Kelley.

Kohlmeier, Louis M., Jr. 1969. *The Regulators*. New York: Harper & Row.

Kolko, Gabriel. 1963. *The Triumph of Conservatism: A Reinterpretation of American History, 1900–1916*. Glencoe, Ill.: Free Press.

Kolko, Gabriel. 1965. *Railroads and Regulation, 1877–1916*. Princeton, N.J.: Princeton University Press.

Krislov, Samuel. 1979. "Debating on Bargaining." 13 *Law and Society Review* 573.

Krooss, Herman E. 1955. *American Economic Development*. Englewood Cliffs, N.J.: Prentice-Hall.

Kuehnl, George J. 1959. *The Wisconsin Business Corporation*. Madison: University of Wisconsin Press.

Ladinsky, Jack; Stewart Macaulay; and Jill Anderson. 1979. *The Milwaukee Dispute Mapping Project*. Madison: University of Wisconsin Law School.

Laitos, Jan S. 1980. *A Legal-Economic History of Air Pollution Controls*. Arlington, Va.: Carrollton Press.

Landis, James M. 1926. "Congressional Power of Investigation." 40 *Harvard Law Review* 153.

Landis, James M. 1938. *Administrative Process*. New Haven: Yale University Press.

Larkin, Paschal. 1930. *Property in the Eighteenth Century*. Dublin: Cork University Press.

Larson, Arthur. 1952. *The Law of Workmen's Compensation*. 3 vols. Albany, N.Y.: Matthew Bender Co.

Laurent, Francis W. 1959. *The Business of a Trial Court*. Madison: University of Wisconsin Press.

Lekachman, Robert. 1966. *the Age of Keynes*. New York: Random House.

Lempert, Richard O. 1978. "More Tales of Two Courts." 13 *Law and Society Review* 91.

Letwin, William. 1965. *Law and Economic Policy in America: The Evolution of the Sherman Antitrust Act*. New York: Random House.

Levy, Leonard W. 1967. *The Law of the Commonwealth and Chief Justice Shaw*. New York: Harper Torchbooks.

Lief, Alfred, ed. 1941. *The Brandeis Guide to the Modern World*. Boston: Little, Brown & Co.

Lindblom, Charles. 1977. *Politics and Markets*. New York: Basic Books.

Linde, Hans A., and George Bunn. 1976. *Legislative and Administrative Processes*. Mineola, N.Y.: Foundation Press.

Livermore, Shaw. 1939. *Early American Land Companies*. New York: Commonwealth Fund.

Llewellyn, Karl N. 1939. Review of Prausnitz, *the Standardization of Commercial Contracts in English and Continental Law*. 52 *Harvard Law Review* 700.

Llewellyn, Karl N. 1960. *The Common Law Tradition: Deciding Appeals*. Boston: Little, Brown & Co.

Locke, John. 1946. *The Second Treatise of Civil Government*. Ed. J. W. Gough. Oxford: Basil Blackwell.

Lowi, Theodore J. 1969. *The End of Liberalism*. New York: W. W. Norton & Co.

Lynd, Robert S., and Helen Merrell Lynd. 1929. *Middletown*. New York: Harcourt, Brace & Co.

Lyon, Levertt S.; Myron W. Watkins; and Victor Abramson. 1939–40. *Government and Economic Life*. 2 vols. Washington, D.C.: Brookings Institution.

McAllister, Breck P. 1938. "Lord Hale and Business Affected with a Public Interest." In *Selected Essays on Constitutional Law*. Vol. 2. Chicago: Foundation Press.

Macaulay, Stewart. 1963. "Non-Contractual Relations in Business: A Preliminary Study." 28 *American Sociological Review* 55.

Macaulay, Stewart. 1966. *Law and the Balance of Power: The Automobile Manufacturers and Their Dealers*. New York: Russell Sage Foundation.

Macaulay, Stewart. 1979. "Lawyers and Consumer Protection Laws." 14 *Law and Society Review* 115.

McCraw, Thomas K. 1975. "Regulation in America: A Review Article." 49 *Business History Review* 159.

McIntosh, W. 1978. "Litigation in the St. Louis Trial Courts of General Jurisdiction: The Effects of Socio-Economic Change." Paper presented at the 1978 annual meeting of the American Political Science Association, New York City, 1978.

MacIver, Robert M. 1948. *The More Perfect Union*. New York: Macmillan Co.

McKean, Dayton D. 1938. *Pressures on the Legislature of New Jersey*. New York: Columbia University Press.

McKenzie, R. D. 1934. "The Rise of Metropolitan Communities." In President's Research Committee on Social Trends, *Recent Social Trends in the United States*. New York: Whittlesey House, McGraw-Hill Book Co.

McLaughlin, Andrew C. 1936. *A Constitutional History of the United States*. New York: D. Appleton-Century Co.

Malone, Dumas. 1948. *Jefferson and His Time: Jefferson the Virginian*. Boston: Little, Brown & Co.

Malone, Dumas. 1951. *Jefferson and the Rights of Man*. Boston: Little, Brown & Co.

Mann, Horace. 1949. "The Importance of Universal, Free Public Education" (1867). In *The People Shall Judge*. Vol. 1. Chicago: University of Chicago Press.

Mason, Alpheus T. 1946. *Brandeis: A Free Man's Life*. New York: Viking Press.

Mayhew, David R. 1974. *Congress: The Electoral Connection*. New Haven: Yale University Press.

Milbrath, Lester W. 1965. *Political Participation*. Chicago: Rand McNally & Co.

Miller, George H. 1970. *Railroads and the Granger Laws*. Madison: University of Wisconsin Press.

Miller, Merle. 1980. *Lyndon*. New York: G. P. Putnam's Sons.

Moore, Harry H. 1934. "Health and Medical Practice." In President's Research Committee on Social Trends, *Recent Social Trends in the United States*. New York: Whittlesey House, McGraw-Hill Book Co.

Mosher, Frederick C., and Orville F. Poland. 1964. *The Costs of American Government*. New York: Dodd Mead & Co.

Mueller, Willard F. 1970. *A Primer on Monopoly and Competition*. New York: Random House.

Murphy, Earl Finbar. 1961. *Water Purity: A Study in Legal Control of Natural Resources*. Madison: University of Wisconsin Press.

Murphy, Earl Finbar. 1967. *Governing Nature*. Chicago: Quadrangle Books.

Nelson, Richard E.; Morton J. Peck; and Edward D. Kalachek. 1967. *Technology, Economic Growth, and Public Policy*. Washington, D.C.: Brookings Institution.

Nelson, William E. 1975. *Americanization of the Common Law: The Impact of Legal Change on Massachusetts Society, 1760–1830*. Cambridge, Mass.: Harvard University Press.

Ogburn, W. F., and S. C. Gilfillan. 1934. "The Influence of Invention and Discovery." In President's Research Committee on Social Trends,

Recent Social Trends in the United States. New York: Whittlesey House, McGraw-Hill Book Co.

Padover, Saul K., ed. 1943. *The Complete Jefferson.* New York: Duell, Sloan & Pearce.

Parrington, Vernon L. 1927. *Main Currents in American Thought.* Vol. 1, *The Colonial Mind, 1620–1800.* New York: Harcourt, Brace & Co.

Patterson, Edwin W. 1953. *Jurisprudence: Men and Ideas of the Law.* Brooklyn: Foundation Press.

Paul, Randolph E. 1954. *Taxation in the United States.* Boston: Little, Brown & Co.

Penrose, Edith T. 1959. *The Theory of the Growth of the Firm.* New York: John Wiley & Sons.

The People Shall Judge: Readings in the Formation of American Policy. 1949. 2 vols. Chicago: University of Chicago Press.

Perlman, Selig. 1949. *A Theory of the Labor Movement.* New York: Augustus M. Kelley.

Polanyi, Karl. 1944. *The Great Transformation.* New York: Farrar & Rinehart.

Potts, C. S. 1926. "Power of Legislative Bodies to Punish for Contempt." 74 *University of Pennsylvania Law Review* 691, 780.

Pound, Roscoe. 1909. "Liberty of Contract." 18 *Yale Law Journal* 454.

Pound, Roscoe. 1938. *The Formative Era of American Law.* Boston: Little, Brown & Co.

Pound, Roscoe. 1940. "The Economic Interpretation of the Law of Torts." 53 *Harvard Law Review* 365.

Pound, Roscoe. 1959. *Jurisprudence.* 5 vols. St. Paul, Minn.: West Publishing Co.

Powell, Richard P. 1949–61. *The Law of Real Property.* Rev. ed. 10 vols. New York: Matthew Bender.

Price, Don K. 1954. *Government and Science: Their Dynamic Relation in American Democracy.* New York: New York University Press.

Price, Don K. 1965. *The Scientific Estate.* Cambridge, Mass.: Belknap Press of Harvard University Press.

Prosser, William L. 1971. *Handbook of Torts.* 4th ed. St. Paul, Minn.: West Publishing Co.

Rabin, Robert. 1979. *Perspectives on the Administrative Process.* Boston: Little, Brown & Co.

Radin, Max. 1936. *On Anglo-American Legal History.* St. Paul, Minn.: West Publishing Co.

Robinson, Richard. 1956. "Interests and Institutions Reflected in Wisconsin Penal Statutes." 1956 *Wisconsin Law Review* 154.

Rohrbough, Malcolm. 1948. *The Land Office Business: The Settlement and Administration of American Public Lands, 1789–1837*. Oxford University Press.

Roosevelt, Theodore. 1925. *An Autobiography*. New York: Charles Scribner's Sons.

Rosenberg, Charles E. 1962. *The Cholera Years*. Chicago: University of Chicago Press.

Rossiter, Clinton. 1964. *Alexander Hamilton and the Constitution*. New York: Harcourt, Brace & World.

Rostow, Eugene V. 1959. *Planning for Freedom: The Public Law of American Capitalism*. New Haven: Yale University Press.

Rottschaefer, Henry. 1939. *Handbook of American Constitutional Law*. St. Paul, Minn.: West Publishing Co.

Ruhnka, J., and S. Weller. 1978. *Small Claims Courts: A National Examination*. Williamsburg, Va.: National Center for State Courts.

Schattschneider, E. E. 1935. *Politics, Pressures, and the Tariff*. New York: Prentice-Hall.

Scheiber, Harry N. 1969. *Ohio Canal Era: A Case Study of Government and the Economy, 1820–1861*. Athens, Ohio: Ohio University Press.

Scheiber, Harry N. 1978. "Property Law, Expropriation, and Resource Allocation by Government, 1789–1910." In Lawrence M. Friedman and Harry N. Scheiber, eds., *American Law and the Constitutional Order*. Cambridge, Mass.: Harvard University Press.

Schlatter, Richard. 1951. *Private Property: The History of an Idea*. New Brunswick, N.J.: Rutgers University Press.

Schumpeter, Joseph A. 1947. *Capitalism, Socialism, and Democracy*. 2d ed. New York: Harper & Brothers.

Seagle, William. 1941. *The Quest for Law*. New York: Alfred A. Knopf.

Seidman, Joel. 1967. Foreword to *Abraham Bismo, Union Pioneer*. Madison: University of Wisconsin Press.

Shonfield, Andrew. 1965. *Modern Capitalism*. New York: Oxford University Press.

Simpson, A.W.B. 1979. "The Horwitz Thesis and the History of Contracts." 46 *University of Chicago Law Review* 533.

Skilton, Robert H. 1961. "Field Warehousing as a Financing Device." 1961 *Wisconsin Law Review* 221.

Skilton, Robert H. 1963. "Tradition and Change: The Law of Mortgages on Merchandise." 1963 *Wisconsin Law Review* 359.

Smith, Adam. 1926–30. *An Inquiry into the Nature and Causes of the Wealth of Nations*. 2 vols. New York: E. P. Dutton & Co.

Smith, Bradford. 1952, 1954. *A Dangerous Freedom*. Philadelphia: J. B. Lippincott Co.

Smith, Dan Throop. 1961. *Federal Tax Reform*. New York: McGraw-Hill Book Co.

Smith, Henry Nash. 1950. *Virgin Land*. Cambridge, Mass.: Harvard University Press.

Smith, Walter B. 1953. *Economic Aspects of the Second Bank of the United States*. Cambridge, Mass.: Harvard University Press.

Sobel, Robert. 1965. *The Big Board: A History of the New York Stock Exchange*. New York: Free Press.

Solberg, Erling D. 1961. *New Laws for New Forests*. Madison: University of Wisconsin Press.

Solo, Robert A. 1967. *Economic Organization and Social Systems*. Indianapolis: Bobbs-Merrill Co.

Stein, Herbert. 1969. *The Fiscal Revolution in America*. Chicago: University of Chicago Press.

Stern, Philip M. 1962. *The Great Treasury Raid*. New York: Random House.

Stetson, Francis Lynde. 1917. "Preparation of Corporate Bonds, Mortgages, Collateral Trusts, and Debenture Indentures." In Francis Lynde Stetson *et al.*, *Some Legal Phases of Corporate Financing, Reorganization, and Regulation*. New York: Macmillan Co.

Stewart, Richard. 1975. "The Reformation of American Administrative Law." 88 *Harvard Law Review* 1667.

Stone, Christopher D. 1972. "Should Trees Have Standing? Toward Legal Rights for Natural Objects." 45 *Southern California Law Review* 450.

Stone, Christopher D. 1975. *Where the Law Ends: The Social Control of Corporate Behavior*. New York: Harper & Row.

Sumner, William Graham. 1947. "What Social Classes Owe to Each Other" (1883). In Louis M. Hacker and Helen S. Zahler, eds., *The Shaping of the American Tradition*. Vol. 2. New York: Columbia University Press.

Surrey, Stanley. 1957. "The Congress and the Tax Lobbyists: How Special Tax Provisions Get Enacted." 70 *Harvard Law Review* 1145.

Sutherland, Arthur E. 1965. *Constitutionalism in America*. New York: Blaisdell Publishing Co.

Sutherland, Edwin H., and C. E. Gehlke. 1934. "Crime and Punishment." In President's Research Committee on Social Trends, *Recent*

Social Trends in the United States. New York: Whittlesey House, McGraw-Hill Book Co.

Sutton, Francis X.; Seymour E. Harris; Carl Kaysen; and James Tobin. 1956. *The American Business Creed.* Cambridge, Mass.: Harvard University Press.

Syndenstricker, Edgar. 1934. "The Vitality of the American People." In President's Research Committee on Social Trends, *Recent Social Trends in the United States.* New York: Whittlesey House, McGraw-Hill Book Co.

Thorelli, Hans B. 1955. *The Federal Antitrust Policy.* Baltimore: Johns Hopkins Press.

Thurman, Kay Ellen. 1966. "The Married Women's Property Acts." LL.M. thesis, University of Wisconsin Law School.

Thurow, Lester C. 1980. *The Zero-Sum Society.* New York: Basic Books.

Tocqueville, Alexis de. 1945. *Democracy in America.* Ed. Phillips Bradley. 2 vols. New York: Alfred A. Knopf.

Treiber, William F. 1965. "The Federal Reserve System after Fifty Years." 20 *The Business Lawyer* 247.

Trescott, Paul B. 1963. *Financing American Enterprise.* New York: Harper & Row.

Tribe, Laurence H. 1978. *American Constitutional Law.* Mineola, N.Y.: Foundation Press.

Truman, David B. 1951. *The Governmental Process.* New York: Alfred A. Knopf.

Turner, James S. 1970. *The Chemical Feast.* New York: Grossman Publishers.

Underwood, Kenneth Wilson. 1957. *Protestant and Catholic: Religious and Social Interaction in an Industrial Community.* Boston: Beacon Press.

Walker, Harvey. 1934. *Law Making in the United States.* New York: Ronald Press Co.

Wall, Joseph F. 1970. Andrew Carnegie. New York: Oxford University Press.

Wanner, Craig. 1974. "The Public Ordering of Private Relations." 8 *Law and Society Review* 421.

Warren, Charles. 1913. "The Progressiveness of the United States Supreme Court." 13 *Columbia Law Review* 294.

Warren, Charles. 1928. *The Making of the Constitution.* Boston: Little, Brown & Co.

Warren, Edward H. 1929. *Corporate Advantages without Incorporation.* New York: Baker Voorhis Co.

Wechsler, Herbert. 1954. "The Political Safeguards of Federalism: The Role of the States in the Composition and Selection of the National Government." 54 *Columbia Law Review* 543.

Weeks, O. Douglas. 1938. "Legislative Power Versus Delegated Legislative Power." In *Selected Essays on Constitutional Law.* Vol. 4. Chicago: Foundation Press.

Wheeler, George. 1973. *Pierpont Morgan and Friends.* Englewood Cliffs, N.J.: Prentice-Hall.

White, Leonard D. 1934. "Public Administration." In President's Research Committee on Social Trends, *Recent Social Trends in the United States.* New York: Whittlesey House, McGraw-Hill Book Co.

Wiebe, Robert J. 1962. *Businessmen and Reform: A Study of the Progressive Movement.* Cambridge, Mass.: Harvard University Press.

Wiley, Malcolm M., and Stuart A. Rice. 1934. "The Agencies of Communication." In President's Research Committee on Social Trends, *Recent Social Trends in the United States.* New York: Whittlesey House, McGraw-Hill Book Co.

Williams, Robin M., Jr. 1951. *American Society.* New York: Alfred A. Knopf.

Woll, Peter. 1960. "Informal Administrative Adjudication: Summary of Findings." 7 *University of California at Los Angeles Law Review* 436.

Wood, Gordon S. 1972. *The Creation of the American Republic, 1776–1787.* New York: W. W. Norton & Co.

Wooddy, Carroll H. 1934. "The Growth of Governmental Functions." In President's Research Committee on Social Trends, *Recent Social Trends in the United States.* New York: Whittlesey House, McGraw-Hill Book Co.

Woodhouse, A. S. P., ed. 1974. *Puritanism and Liberty.* Chicago: University of Chicago Press.

Wright, Benjamin F., Jr. 1938. *The Contract Clause of the Constitution.* Cambridge, Mass.: Harvard University Press.

Index

193

JACKET DESIGNED BY IRVING PERKINS ASSOCIATES
COMPOSED BY THE COMPOSING ROOM, KIMBERLY, WISCONSIN
MANUFACTURED BY THE BANTA COMPANY, MENASHA, WISCONSIN
TEXT AND DISPLAY LINES ARE SET IN SABON

ᵘ⨆ᵘ

Library of Congress Cataloging in Publication Data
Hurst, James Willard, 1910–
Law and markets in United States history.
(The Curti lectures; 1981)
Bibliography: p. 173–191.
Includes index.
1. Trade regulation—United States. 2. Commercial
law—United States. I. Title. II. Series.
KF1600.H87   343.73'08   81–69822
ISBN 0–299–09050–7   347.3038   AACR2
ISBN 0–299–09054–X (pbk.)